On the Poems of Tennyson

ON THE POEMS OF

By WARD HELLSTROM

University of Florida Press/*Gainesville*

Library of Congress Cataloging in Publication Data
Hellstrom, Ward, 1930–
  On the poems of Tennyson.
  Includes bibliographical references.
  1. Tennyson, Alfred Tennyson, Baron, 1809–1892.
I. Title.
PR5588.H43   821'.8   72–150654
ISBN 0–8130–0322–9

Designed by Gary Gore

Printed in Florida

For Royal A. Gettmann

Preface

LIKE much Victorian, Tennyson suffered in the first half of the twentieth century, the victim of an age bent upon repudiating the Victorian world. Because he was popular, was laureate, and was wealthy as a result of his poetry, he suffered further at the hands of an age given to the proposition that the best poets a "fit audience find, though few." Most of all perhaps he suffered because of his friends—the Tennyson societies made up of ministers of the gospel and spinsters; the English and American professors of literature who, in the early decades of this century, spoke of Tennyson as philosopher and Tennyson as religious teacher; and even his own son, whose 800-page memoir has done much to perpetuate the laureate image. The action of these friends brought inevitable reaction.

At a time when Irving Babbitt and T. E. Hulme were unable to counteract the singular appeal of the Romantics, Tennyson went under as a Victorian and emerged as a Romantic. In the first important book after Hallam Tennyson's *Memoir* (1897), Harold Nicolson attempted to save Tennyson in the only way perhaps that he could have been saved at the time. In *Tennyson: Aspects of His Life, Character and Poetry* (1923) Nicolson isolated those poems which he thought most Romantic—i.e., most emotional—rejected out of hand those in which Tennyson appeared to think, and concluded that "of all poets, Tennyson should be read carelessly or not at all." Not only did Nicolson fix the canon for future anthologists, but he set the direction for much future criticism when, as his subtitle indicates, Tennyson's poetry ran a poor third to aspects of his life and character.

If Nicolson's book was an important book and a good book for 1923, saving at least those poems which Nicolson liked and which his age was most likely to accept, it nevertheless led to unfortunate consequences. It was Nicolson's list of acceptable poems, for example, which apparently determined W. H. Auden's choice in *A Selection from the Poems of Alfred Lord Tennyson* (1944) and which probably led to Auden's lamentable comment about Tennyson—"he had the finest ear, perhaps, of any English poet, he was also undoubtedly the stupidest." And Nicolson's critical approach, biographical and psychological, has set the tenor for much modern criticism.

I have tried in this book to address myself to the poems—to what they say and how they say it—and have not been interested in Tennyson's life or his psyche. That is, I have not used the poems to try to understand the man, an endeavor which has occupied many critics. I am less interested in what Tennyson may subconsciously have felt than in what he apparently thought and said. I have not attempted to establish and prove a thesis, though there are some patterns and a consistency which do emerge from a study of all the poems. My purpose has been only to give a reading of individual poems and attention to the way they relate to other poems rather than to Tennyson himself. Some very good poems are noticeably absent from this study—e.g., *Ode on the Death of the Duke of Wellington,* the songs from *The Princess,* and *Rizpah* —because I felt I had little critical contribution to make to them.

Tennyson is not, of course, a Romantic, but a Victorian. And it is here that his relationship with the Liberal Anglicans is perhaps most helpful. Though I often illustrate Tennyson with Liberal Anglican thought, thought with which he was certainly familiar, I have not meant to establish a source for Tennyson. I have used the Liberal Anglicans as discursive analogues for what I think Tennyson is saying poetically. If, as I believe, his thinking is closely analogous to that of the Liberal Anglicans, Tennyson belongs in the most modern theological and historical tradition of the Victorian period. And this is an aspect of his art which has gone until now unexamined.

I am indebted to the Graduate School of the University of Florida and to the Humanities Council of the College of Arts and Sciences for summer grants which allowed me to complete this study. I wish also to acknowledge the courteous assistance of Carol Quinn, Sherman L. Butler, and the staff of the University of

Florida Libraries, and Mr. A. Halcrow, sublibrarian of Trinity College Library, Cambridge, who provided me with a microfilm of the Trinity MSS. As always, I am indebted to Thomas R. Preston, who long ago encouraged my interest in Tennyson. It is a pleasure to thank my students, who listened to me with patience, and my colleagues—John T. Fain, Richard A. Dwyer, and William Ruff—who read parts of this study. My special thanks go to Cecil Y. Lang for his careful and thorough reading of the entire manuscript and for his most helpful comments and suggestions. And finally I should like to thank my wife and children for their forbearance and to remember Robert A. Johnson, for whom I have always had the greatest regard.

W. H.

Contents

On the Poems of Tennyson

1. Some Early Poems

*T*HE Romantics regularly concerned themselves in their poetry with the role of the poet; their Victorian successors as regularly concerned themselves with the nature of poetic life. In other words, the Victorian poets—Arnold, Browning, and Tennyson, for example—were not concerned simply with what a poet does, but with where a poet lives. Arnold phrased the problem this way:

> Ah! two desires toss about
> The poet's feverish blood.
> One drives him to the world without,
> And one to solitude.[1]

The question is one of involvement or isolation, and Arnold proposed various answers to it. Empedocles, for example, shrinking from the twin torments of the world and solitude, chooses death to "Bring him to poise." [2] But Arnold's speakers and Arnold himself more regularly choose isolation—in *Self-Dependence*, in *Resignation*, in *Stanzas in Memory of the Author of Obermann*, for example. And the images which Arnold regularly used to describe the poet further clarify his choice: Shakespeare is a mountain with its dwelling place in heaven and only "the cloudy border of his base / [Spared] to the foiled searching of mortality,"

---

1. *Stanzas in Memory of the Author of Obermann* (93–96). *The Poems of Matthew Arnold*, ed. Kenneth Allott (New York, 1965). All quotations from Arnold's poems are from this text.

2. *Empedocles on Etna* (II, i, 220–34). Arnold's withdrawal of the poem from the 1853 edition of the poems suggests that he may not have been happy with Empedocles' solution, though, as the "Preface" makes clear, there were other reasons for the deletion.

or the poet is one who "leaves his kind, o'erleaps their pen, / And flees the common life of men." [3] Browning, on the other hand, clearly and consistently chooses involvement rather than isolation, not only for the poet, but for all men. Abt Vogler finds as his resting place "The C Major of this life," and the successful Fra Lippo Lippi, who comes down into the streets, is opposed to the failure Andrea del Sarto, who remains isolated in his "melancholy little house."

Tennyson, like Arnold, addressed himself to the aesthetic-moral choice between isolation and involvement and saw, like Empedocles, that such a choice might bring with it the further choice between life and death. And, like Browning, Tennyson, at least in the years after 1830, consistently endorsed the choice of life over death and involvement over isolation. But in this opinion I am joined by relatively few of Tennyson's critics. Others have well recognized the alternatives proposed in the early poems, but they find often in them a psychological attraction to isolation and death which belies any conscious moral commitment to involvement and life. Poems thus judged often appear ambivalent, confused, and unsuccessful. While I do not wish to suggest that withdrawal or even death might not have had an attraction for Tennyson, I find neither ambivalence nor confusion in these poems. I am concerned only with what the poems say, or what they seem to me to say, not with what Tennyson may have felt. In limiting my discussion in this chapter to eight poems, I have necessarily eliminated many poems worthy of critical attention.[4]

*

The earliest poetry of Tennyson was to a considerable extent indebted to some of his Romantic predecessors. Byron was an early and short-lived influence, Keats and Shelley later and more long-lasting. As this indebtedness has been traced by others,[5] I do

3. *Shakespeare* and *Resignation* (211–12) .

4. There are of course other superior poems of this period not discussed, for example, *Mariana, Oenone, Morte d'Arthur,* and the political songs; some of these as well as some of the inferior early poems will be discussed by way of illustration in later chapters.

5. See, for example, Jerome Hamilton Buckley, *Tennyson: The Growth of a Poet* (Boston, 1965) , p. 9 et passim (hereafter cited as *Tennyson*) ; Patricia Ball,

not intend to deal with it at any length here. Two poems, however, which appeared in *Poems, Chiefly Lyrical* (1830) and were reprinted essentially unchanged in *Poems* (1842), are interesting in part because they show Tennyson confronting an essential Romantic question—the nature and role of the poet—and confronting it in a very derivative way, but more importantly because they reflect a position, apparently held in 1830, which Tennyson consistently repudiates after 1832.

The first, *The Poet,* one of Tennyson's more successful early poems, is really a variation on a metaphor by Shelley. In the poem, "the viewless arrows" of the poet's thoughts are first likened to "Indian reeds blown from his silver tongue." [6] They then are transformed into the arrowlike seeds of the dandelion, which blow abroad to take root, reproduce the mother plant, and become

> A flower all gold,
>
> And bravely furnished all abroad to fling
> The wingèd shafts of truth,
> To throng with stately blooms the breathing spring
> Of Hope and Youth.

The arrow-seeds of Tennyson's poem carry the same metaphoric weight as the dead leaves of Shelley's *Ode to the West Wind*. In both poems there is the same enjambment of lines across stanzas, a reflex perhaps of the same conceptions of a convoluted natural process. There is the same hope for spring, the same confidence in the validity of the poet's insight, essentially the same dominant metaphor. Moreover, the description of Wisdom in the final quatrain of *The Poet* assigns to poets essentially the same role as that assigned to them in Shelley's *The Defence of Poetry*, that of "the unacknowledged legislators of the world":

"Tennyson and the Romantics," *Victorian Poetry*, 1 (1963): 7–16; George Ford, *Keats and the Victorians* (New Haven, 1944); H. N. Fairchild, "Tennyson and Shelley," *Times Literary Supplement*, 11 January 1947, p. 23; Gerhard Joseph, *Tennysonian Love* (Minneapolis, 1969), pp. 19–24 et passim.

6. I have used the Christopher Ricks edition of *The Poems of Tennyson* (London, 1969) (hereafter cited as *Poems*). I have numbered the lines in my text of the relatively long poems and have italicized the titles of all poems for the reader's convenience.

> . . . . No sword
> Of wrath her right arm whirled,
> But one poor poet's scroll, and with *his* word
> She shook the world.[7]

The poem is clearly imitative and so, I suggest, is the Romantic assertion it makes. The poem asks, what is the role of the poet? The answer advanced by the young Tennyson is really Shelley's answer and not ultimately the answer of Tennyson himself. The poem is a simple, straightforward, and positive celebration of the proper role of the poet, which Tennyson was apparently capable of producing only before 1832.

The second poem, *The Poet's Mind,* is much inferior to the first [8] and owes more to Coleridge [9] than to Shelley. In the poem, the poet's mind is described as "Flowing like a crystal river," similar perhaps to the "sacred river" of *Kubla Khan.* Moreover, the "Dark-browed sophist" is warned to "come not anear" because "All the place is holy ground," [10] as in Coleridge's poem the "savage place" inhabited by the poet is "holy and enchanted" and men must beware. In both poems, there is a garden from which leaps a fountain—in Tennyson "Like sheet lightning, / Ever brightening / With a low melodious thunder," and in Cole-

7. George O. Marshall, Jr., suggests also that "the similarity of Tennyson's conception to that of Shelley's *Defense of Poetry* [*sic*] is obvious, though the *Defense* was not published until ten years after Tennyson's poem" (*A Tennyson Handbook* [New York, 1963], p. 38 [hereafter cited as *Handbook*]) ; see Marshall's "Tennyson's 'The Poet': Mis-seeing Shelley Plain," *Philological Quarterly,* 40 (1961): 156–57. Ricks (*Poems,* 222*nn*) makes no mention of Shelley but twice compares Tennyson to Keats.

8. *The Poet's Mind* was one of the poems of the 1830 volume selected for ridicule, and with some justification, by "Christopher North" in his *Blackwood's* article (May, 1832), p. 727, reprinted in J. D. Jump, ed., *Tennyson: The Critical Heritage* (London, New York, 1967), pp. 50–65.

9. See Hallam Tennyson, *Alfred Lord Tennyson: A Memoir* (London, 1899), p. 42 (hereafter cited as *Memoir*): "Coleridge, indeed, for whose prose my father never much cared, but to whose poetry, especially 'Kubla Khan,' 'The Ancient Mariner,' and 'Christabel,' he was devoted. . . ." John Churton Collins finds Tennyson's *Recollections of the Arabian Nights* in terms of tone and style "little more than an echo of Coleridge's *Kubla Khan* and *Lewti*" (*Illustrations of Tennyson* [London, 1891], p. 28), but Collins is notoriously inaccurate in his ascriptions. See H. P. Sucksmith, "Tennyson on the Nature of His Own Poetic Genius," *Renaissance and Modern Studies,* 11 (1967): 84–89, for an account of Tennyson's rejection of various Collins ascriptions.

10. In the 1830 version, the line read, "The poet's mind is holy ground."

ridge one "Amid whose swift half-intermitted burst / Huge frag-
ments vaulted like rebounding hail." More important, however,
than possible echoes of *Kubla Khan* in *The Poet's Mind* are certain affinities between the conceptions of the nature of the poet
in the two poems. In both poems, the poet's mind is described
as a holy place beyond common apprehension, and the poet is at
once mysterious and mystical.[11] But it is a derivative conception
of the poet which Tennyson, if he ever held it himself, held only
temporarily. A far more important poem in the Tennyson canon,
The Palace of Art, begins like *The Poet's Mind* and *Kubla Khan*,
but it does so in order finally to repudiate the position taken in
those two poems.

Richard Trench's remark "Tennyson, we cannot live in art"[12]
is well known and has long been associated with *The Palace of
Art* (1832, 1842), and the dedicatory epistle "To ———" makes
clear that the moral of the poem is summed up in Trench's statement (or at least Tennyson thought so). Recent critics, however,
have found the poem ambiguous and have either labeled it a
failure or have been unhappy with the conclusion. One critic
finds the poem "depicting the sensuous pleasures of the soul" a
failure not only because it is too didactic but because it is subject
to a "two-directional pull." The question of isolation or involvement, therefore, "emotionally . . . remains unanswered," and
"The poem, consequently, does not move us at all because the
poetry belongs to the palace and not to the moral."[13] Another
critic, less condemnatory, finds "the cottage in the vale" a "vague
objective" and the "extent to which [the soul] will ever recognize
the claims of society" to be "quite uncertain"; and he fears that
"even the cottage life may prove another hedonistic adventure, an
exploitation of simplicity as relief from excessive ornament."[14]
A final critic finds the ending of the poem ambiguous because
the palace is not destroyed and suggests that "Presumably, then,

11. The language of another early Tennyson poem, *The Mystic,* is similar.
Indeed, both the poet and the mystic seem very much alike in their distance
from common men, their mysterious nature, and their superiority in these poems
of 1830.

12. *Memoir,* p. 100.

13. Clyde Ryals, *Theme and Symbol in Tennyson's Poems to 1850* (Philadel-
phia, 1964), p. 84 (hereafter cited as *Theme and Symbol*).

14. Buckley, *Tennyson,* p. 53.

we are to believe that Tennyson would not altogether discredit the life of the imagination, but rather would insinuate that the artist must become aware of the responsibility to communicate his insights."[15]

Before judging the success of the poem as a whole or of its ending, one must determine what kind of a palace it is which the soul must leave. It is clearly not a palace of "the sensuous pleasures of the soul." An examination of the stanzas rejected in revision of the poem suggests that Tennyson wished specifically to avoid the "sensuous pleasures." As W. J. Rolfe pointed out, "The poet wisely decided to allow his luxurious 'soul' none but intellectual joys."[16] It is, on the contrary, a palace of art; and it is not, of course, destroyed, nor should one expect the poet to counsel its destruction. The question in the poem is not whether one should or should not practice art, or whether art should or should not be destroyed, but what kind of art a poet should practice, or, more precisely, what kind of poet a poet should be.

Like *The Poet's Mind*, *The Palace of Art* echoes *Kubla Khan*, but in the later poem more specifically and perhaps more pointedly. Tennyson's "lordly pleasure-house" (1) is perhaps too close to Coleridge's "stately pleasure-dome" to be mere accident. Moreover, the description of the external palace is very like that of the palace of the Khan. Instead of "walls and towers" in Coleridge, we have "rangèd ramparts" (6) in Tennyson; instead of "spots of greenery," there are "green courts" (25); instead of a "chasm" from which is forced "a mighty fountain," we have a "golden gorge of dragons" (23) from which spouts forth "A flood of fountain-foam" (24); instead of "many an incense-bearing tree," we have "A cloud of incense" (39); where in Coleridge there is ice, in Tennyson there is frost (52). The echoes of *Kubla Khan* are strong in *The Palace of Art*,[17] I think, not because Tennyson

15. E. D. H. Johnson, *The Alien Vision in Victorian Poetry* (Princeton, 1952), p. 12 (hereafter cited as *Alien Vision*).

16. Ed., *The Complete Poetical Works of Tennyson* (Cambridge, Mass., 1898), p. 803n (hereafter cited as *Works*). In line 216 Tennyson specifically describes the "soul's" throne as "intellectual."

17. Andy P. Antippas, in "Tennyson, Hallam, and *The Palace of Art*," *Victorian Poetry*, 5 (1967): 295, juxtaposes Tennyson and Hallam: "While Tennyson evoked the poetical landscape of Coleridge: 'I built my soul a lordly pleasure-house' (1. 1), Hallam insisted on less exotic sanctuaries: 'Thy Palaces and pleasure-

is imitating Coleridge as he had perhaps imitated him in *The Poet's Mind* or as he had imitated Shelley in *The Poet*, but because he wishes to begin with the Coleridgean conception of the poet in order to reject it in the poem.[18]

Coleridge seems to be describing the poet as a man who plunges to the depths of his imagination, who lives in isolation on holy ground, a man of whom men must beware; the description is a description of what Keats referred to as "the Wordsworthian, or egotistical sublime; which is a thing per se, and stands alone." It is both the isolation and the egotism of the Coleridgean poet that are rejected in *The Palace of Art*. The poet may not isolate himself in such a palace because, as Tennyson tells us in the introductory epistle, equally important to the beautiful is the good. He cannot divorce himself from men and seek to live as a god alone with beauty, because in so doing he is guilty of pride. We do not have to wait until the final stanza of the poem for Tennyson's rejection of the palace as a place where one can dwell in isolation; we do not even have to wait until the final section (213–96), where we learn that in the fourth year the soul fell. The preceding section (129–212) is full of the language of hubris: the soul speaks of her isolation as "God-like" (197), while men are no more than "darkening droves of swine" (199); she sits "as God" (211); and she "prate[s]" "of the rising from the dead, / As hers by right of full-accomplished Fate" (205–7). She is guilty of the sin of Satan and Eve; she is guilty of "serpent pride" (257), for she would be a god. Her sin is not that she loved beauty or that she loved knowledge, but that she dwelt in a palace of art isolated from mankind. The soul's sin, as the introductory epistle tells us, is that she has shut Love out. Like the Ancient Mariner in a quite differently conceived Coleridgean poem, the soul must learn to love, and so she comes down from her palace to "a cottage in the vale" (291).

---

domes to me / Are matter of strange thought.' . . ." Joseph Sendry in "'The Palace of Art' Revisited," *Victorian Poetry*, 4 (1966): 149–62, the most extended treatment of the poem, finds in the poem a "medley of Biblical allusions." Ricks, in *Poems*, suggests for comparison more than thirty sources, analogues, or parallels, but nowhere Coleridge.

18. I do not wish to restrict Coleridge to the conception of the poet found in *Kubla Khan*, but only to suggest that it is this conception of the poet which Tennyson appears to reject.

To conclude that *The Palace of Art* "does not move us at all because the poetry belongs to the palace and not to the moral" is, possibly, to misread the poem. If the poetry belongs to the palace, surely the moral belongs to it also, for it is in the palace that we see the nature and extent of the soul's sin. The return to the cottage in the vale is adequately prepared for in the poem, as the nature of the sin has determined the method of expiation: the prideful soul which had isolated itself from men must return to the world of men. On the other hand, I do not think one need fear that the cottage in the vale may prove to be "another hedonistic adventure, an exploitation of simplicity as relief from excessive ornament." The escape from the palace is not an escape from excessive ornament but an escape from excessive pride, an escape from the isolation, not the art, of the palace. The soul retires to the cottage, not to find simplicity, but to enter the world and perhaps to find love. Nor do I think there is any "two-directional pull" here, if by two-directional pull is meant an ambivalence on the poet's part toward the determination of the soul to leave the palace. Clearly the soul's salvation depends upon a return to the world. The palace, however, must not be destroyed because it is a palace of *art*, and the soul is both soul and artist. Art must be neither a refuge for the superior being from "the darkening droves of swine," nor a palace from which the poet as superior being can legislate for mankind. The palace of art is a palace of beauty to which others may be brought by the proper kind of poet, that is, by the poet who loves his fellow men and wishes to bring them to the beautiful.

Tennyson handled essentially the same theme but from a different point of view in *The Lady of Shalott* (1832, 1842). Criticism of the poem differs in the interpretation of details and the conclusions it reaches rather than in its general understanding of the problem which the poem postulates. Most critics agree that the poem deals with the problem of artistic isolation and they are in general accord that the effect of the world may be destructive to the artist. Either the world of direct experience destroys the creative imagination,[19] or human experience may destroy the

19. Johnson, *Alien Vision*, p. 9: "Appropriately, the world which the lady enters has been drained of the color and animation lent by fancy; and the manner of her dying symbolizes the extinction of the vitalizing imagination within her."

artist, though paradoxically love in that experience is highly desirable,[20] or Tennyson's own experience is reflected autobiographically in the poem.[21] Isolation in all these interpretations has some positive value and it is here where my own reading of the poem differs.

The Lady of Shalott lives in a castle of "Four gray walls, and four gray towers" (15) on a "silent isle" (17) surrounded by willow trees. The imagery suggests not only isolation but also a kind of death-in-life. Indeed, an examination of successive revisions of the poem reveals that Tennyson deleted those details which detracted from the somber setting. For example, though the gray walls and towers of the final version still "Overlook a space of flowers" (16), Tennyson has eliminated the roses and rose fence, the "yellowleavèd waterlily" and the "lowhung daffodilly" of the earlier versions.[22] Moreover, the Lady remains in the final version described by the reapers as "the fairy / Lady of Shalott" (35–36), indicating perhaps that they doubt she is human; but the reference to her as singing "Like an angel" is deleted, perhaps because Tennyson does not wish to suggest any positive spiritual value to the Lady's existence. Whatever the reasons for the revisions of the poem, it seems clear that the final version finds the isle less idyllic than earlier ones.

Cf. Joseph, *Tennysonian Love*, p. 49: "The creation of a sensuous art necessitates the artist's separation from normal activity, especially from the common experience of love."

20. Lona Mosk Packer, "Sun and Shadow: The Nature of Experience in Tennyson's 'The Lady of Shalott,'" *Victorian Newsletter*, no. 25 (Spring 1964): 8: "Reality in this poem takes on a specialized meaning: knowledge of truth becomes by way of Christian logic knowledge of love, but more particularly, knowledge of sexual love. And yet the poet is not at all convinced that this kind of human experience may be acquired without destroying the creative capacity of the artist. Paradoxically the liberating 'curse,' which can free the creative personality from a cocoon-like seclusion—one both desired and detested—and bring him into the main current of human life, may at the same time prove his undoing as an artist."

21. Ryals, *Theme and Symbol*, p. 76: "If one wished to see an analogy between the Lady of Shalott and the poet, it might be something like this: Tennyson was happy in his isolation and realized the dangers attendant upon leaving it; but he was being made to feel the necessity for mixing with the world, and so was weighing the possibilities of what the consequences would be if he attempted to reorient his art."

22. See notes on revisions in Rolfe, *Works*, pp. 796–97; Christopher Ricks, "The Tennyson Manuscripts," *TLS*, 21 August 1969, p. 920; or *Poems*, pp. 355–61*nn*.

In her tower the Lady weaves and sings, but not about reality, of which she has no direct experience. And we are reminded, by the Lady's ignorance of reality (as we are expected to be reminded in the poem), of the analogous ignorance on the part of the inhabitants of Plato's cave.[23] Like the benighted cave-dwellers of Plato's allegory, whose conception of reality is limited to the shadows of artificial objects held up before a fire, the Lady of Shalott knows reality only as the reflections of shadows in a mirror.[24] And as in Plato one must go out of the cave of shadows to glimpse the sun of reality even if it means blindness and even if it means death on one's return to his fellow men, so must the Lady leave her world of shadows. Further, when the Lady first faces reality, it appears, as in Plato, as the sun: in Part III, Lancelot, the figure who induces the Lady to confront reality, is associated with the sun. For the first time in the poem, as he rides "The sun came dazzling through the leaves" (75) and "His broad clear brow in sunlight glowed" (100).

The nature of the reality in which Lancelot participates is suggested in many ways by Tennyson. Lancelot is not simply "a virility symbol," though he may be that; nor is the figure on his shield merely "a symbol of sexual dedication." [25] Reality is light and perhaps color, as opposed to shadow.[26] Reality seems also to be holy as suggested by the red-cross knight, symbol of holiness, who kneels on the shield of Lancelot.[27] It is indeed only outside the tower in reality that there is any mention of holiness (as in

23. Mrs. Packer suggests that "the poem cannot be rightly understood without reference to Plato's metaphysical allegory, as Socrates relates in the seventh book of *The Republic*" (p. 7). She goes on, however, to draw different conclusions from mine.

24. Johnson also points out that the Lady of Shalott is twice removed from reality, that her web is "the shadow of a shadow." But he interprets the shadow of a shadow as "an idealized version of the actuality which will destroy her when she meets it face to face" (*Alien Vision*, p. 9). Such an interpretation, of course, reverses the elements of the Platonic allegory, making the shadows the idealization.

25. Packer, p. 7.

26. It is true that the Lady weaves "with colours gay" (38) and that therefore her world is not without color in the tower; but the world which her art imitates is without color if Tennyson means by shadows real shadows rather than images in the mirror.

27. Tennyson changes the shield of Lancelot in the later *Lancelot and Elaine* in the *Idylls of the King* to "azure lions, crowned with gold, / Ramp in the field" (659–60).

the holy carol which the Lady sings) or of God. Art also exists outside in reality—in Lancelot's song and in the Lady's mournful carol—and it exists permanently as opposed to the transitory existence of art in the tower. While the red-cross knight painted on Lancelot's shield "for ever kneeled" (78), the Lady's tapestry in the tower, an art three times removed from reality, is apparently destroyed when the Lady draws upon herself the curse. If there appears to be a kind of permanence in the tower, it is only the permanence of a stasis which is death-in-life. It is outside the tower in reality that eternity exists in art and in "the wave that runs for ever / By the island in the river" (12–13).

It is all this—light, holiness, art, permanence, love—which the Lady chooses because she is "half sick of shadows" (71). Her choice is both a positive choice of the world outside and a rejection of the world inside the tower, and it is her choice which brings upon her the curse. The curse is not, I think, as Jerome Buckley suggests, "the endowment of sensibility that commits her to a vicarious life." [28] She is endowed with that sensibility before the curse ever falls, or at least is forced to live a vicarious existence, and the curse is to be activated only "if she stay / To look down to Camelot" (40–41). The curse, it seems to me, is rather the Edenic curse of mortality and it has all the paradoxical quality of that curse. The curse may kill, but it also frees the Lady, if not from the "cruel immortality" of Tithonus, at least from a kind of death-in-life. It is only by the acceptance of death that the Lady can embrace life. As Tennyson had said in *Love and Death* (published in 1830 and reprinted unchanged in 1842), "Life eminent creates the shade of death." The Lady's choice is

---

28. *Tennyson,* p. 49. Nor do I think that the nature of the curse is clarified in the way Mrs. Packer suggests: "In the 1833 version of *Shalott* the terms of the curse are defined more explicitly:

> No time hath she to sport and play:
> A charmèd web she weaves alway.
> A curse is on her if she stay
> Her weaving, either night or day
>> To look down on Camelot.

The Lady is accursed if she cease her occupation for 'sport and play,' the preliminaries to love, of which the practice has been perfected in the sophisticated court circles of Camelot" (p. 7).

not death but life. There has been no life in the tower and therefore none of the stuff with which the artist must deal; there have
been only the reflections of shadows.

It has been argued that the people of the world outside of
Shalott do not understand the artist and are destructive to her,
and evidence for this is the appearance of the "wellfed wits" of
the 1832 version of the poem, excised by Tennyson in revision. It
is important, however, that it is not the people of Camelot who
destroy her; she dies when she enters life, as all must die when they
enter life, but she also lives for the first time. If the townspeople
do not understand her, Lancelot does and is distinguished from
them:

> But Lancelot mused a little space;
> He said, 'She has a lovely face;
> God in his mercy lend her grace,
>   The Lady of Shalott.' (168–71)

His comment is neither banal nor the result of misunderstanding.
He does understand and he adjudges her lovely, that is, capable
of engendering love. The capacity for giving and receiving love
and the curse of mortality for the first time make the Lady human.
As W. D. Paden says of the poem, "In a very Tennysonian revision
of Faber, the birth of a soul is identified with the coming of love,
and love brings with it the doom of God." [29]

I find it difficult to read the poem as a statement of the
destructive effect of the world on the artist's sensitivity, because
the world of artistic sensitivity in which the Lady lives is so
meaningless, so unreal. Indeed, the unreality of such a world is
intensified by its correspondence to the unreal world of Plato's
cave. And if Matthew Arnold is right, "that poetry is at bottom a
criticism of life; that the greatness of a poet lies in his powerful and
beautiful applications of ideas to life,—to the question: How to
live," can there be justification for the existence of the Lady as

29. *Tennyson in Egypt: A Study of the Imagery in His Earlier Work,* University of Kansas Humanistic Studies, no. 27 (Lawrence, 1942), p. 156n204. Cf. Tennyson's own interpretation as told to Canon Ainger: "The new-born love for something, for some one in the wide world from which she has been so long secluded,
takes her out of the region of shadows into that of realities" (quoted in *Memoir,*
p. 99).

artist in the tower? in an unreal world? An art divorced from reality for Arnold is no art, and Tennyson's early poetry suggests that Tennyson believed the same thing to be true. Moreover, a life divorced from life is no life as Tennyson said in *The Palace of Art* and as he said again in the poem *The Lotos-Eaters* (1832, 1842).

Certainly Tennyson was aware that *The Lotos-Eaters* is the text for which the context is the *Odyssey*. He can therefore expect the reader to be predisposed to reject the position of the mariners, which in the *Odyssey* is dangerous and wrong. He reminds us of this context by opening the poem with Ulysses, who calls his men to courage. After the opening lines, Ulysses no more appears explicitly, but he is implicitly in the poem and provides in part, as we shall see, the context for our understanding of it.

The lotos land is described for us before the choric song as an unreal land, a land of seeming: there "it seemèd always afternoon"; there "the slender stream / Along the cliff to fall and pause and fall did seem"; it is "A land where all things always seemed the same," where "the gushing of the wave / Far far away did seem to mourn and rave," where "if his fellow spake, / His voice was thin, as voices from the grave; / And deep-asleep he seemed," where "Most weary seemed the sea." The land is not only unreal, but it is static rather than permanent,[30] and that stasis suggests death. Voices sound as if they come from the grave. It is a land of swoon and dream and sleep, that sleep which is death's second self.

In the choric song, as others have pointed out, there is an alternation of stanzas, with one devoted to a description of the lotos land and the following to the rationalizations of the mariners. The contrapuntal structure of the stanzas prevents the reader, just as the mariners have been prevented, from being lulled into an acceptance of the lotos land; that is, the reader, like the mariners, is continually drawn away from the island and back to thoughts of the real world by allusion to that world. At the same time, the odd-

30. The static nature of the land is clarified by Tennyson in his revisions of the poem. In place of two lines in the 1832 version, "Above the valley burned the golden moon" and "Three thundercloven thrones of oldest snow," Tennyson substituted in the 1842 version "Full-faced above the valley stood the moon" and "Three silent pinnacles of agèd snow." Action is wisely deleted in revision in favor of stasis.

numbered stanzas, those devoted to the description of the lotos land, belie themselves: they describe not a land of beauty and sensuous pleasure, but a land of overripeness which is the prelude to death, a land where flowers may bloom, but only to fade and fall, where leaves turn yellow and fall, where apples drop in the silent autumn night. The time is not spring, but autumn; the emphasis of the stanzas is not on fruition, but decay.

The even-numbered stanzas—those which deal with the lives of the mariners as opposed to those which deal with their symbolic death, the lotos land—also belie the assertions of the mariners. Most important in this regard is stanza VI, which Tennyson added in 1842, in part presumably to maintain the contrapuntal structure, but more importantly perhaps to clarify the implicit rejection of the mariners' position. I will quote the entire stanza:

Dear is the memory of our wedded lives,
And dear the last embraces of our wives
And their warm tears: but all hath suffered change:
For surely now our household hearths are cold:
Our sons inherit us: our looks are strange:
And we should come like ghosts to trouble joy.
Or else the island princes over-bold
Have eat our substance, and the minstrel sings
Before them of the ten years' war in Troy,
And our great deeds, as half-forgotten things.
Is there confusion in the little isle?
Let what is broken so remain.
The Gods are hard to reconcile:
'Tis hard to settle order once again.
There *is* confusion worse than death,
Trouble on trouble, pain on pain,
Long labour unto agèd breath,
Sore task to hearts worn out by many wars
And eyes grown dim with gazing on the pilot-stars.

This is the stanza in which our recognition of the context of the poem is most important. The evils of Ithaca which the mariners here propose are precisely those which Ulysses must go back to and does go back to rectify. His household hearth is not cold, because Penelope awaits faithfully his return. His son will not inherit him because the island princes eat his substance, and Ulysses must return to drive the island princes out and preserve the inheritance for Telemachus. Ulysses does not come to trouble joy as there is no joy until he comes. It is most certainly hard to settle order once again, but it is the duty of Ulysses to settle that order. If there is confusion worse than death, that confusion is in Ithaca. The context, therefore, contradicts the text. We know that order must be restored and can be restored because Ulysses does it and that such activity is what living requires. What it takes is the courage that Ulysses had called the mariners to at the beginning of the poem.

Two other revisions in the 1842 version of the poem also suggest that Tennyson attempted to clarify in order to avoid misunderstanding. In section VIII, the mariners in the new version feel the necessity to swear an oath to live in the lotos land. If the land is as desirable as they would have us believe, why all the rationalizations and why the necessity of an oath? The substance of the oath also radically distinguishes the revision from the original: in the revision, the mariners are to swear "to live and lie reclined / On the hills like Gods together, careless of mankind" (154–55). There were no Gods in the 1832 version and the inclusion of them here suggests the hubristic nature of the mariners' intent. Their pride is the same serpent pride of the soul in *The Palace of Art,* who desires to be "as God." Quite clearly, it seems to me, both the context and the text of the poem demand condemnation of the mariners. The poem is neither an example of "an acceptance of the desire for escape" on the part of the "Romantic Tennyson," [31] nor does it express, I think, "Tennyson's inclinations toward tranquility and lassitude . . . his desire for dreamful ease." [32] On the contrary, *The Lotos-Eaters* is one of Tennyson's most successful expressions of the rejection of just such desires.

Another poem of the 1842 volumes dealing with the Homeric legend is *Ulysses,* which has been described as "the natural

---

31. Ryals, *Theme and Symbol,* p. 100.

32. Marshall, *Handbook,* p. 71. Cf. Joseph, *Tennysonian Love,* p. 34, who says of the Sisters in *The Hesperides,* "one can already feel in his uneasy praise of their private sensuous garden an indistinct preparation for his equally ambiguous rejection of Lotos-land and the Palace of Art"; or J. B. Steane, *Tennyson* (London, 1966), p. 46: in *The Lotos Eaters, "Officially* he is writing a denunciation; *creatively* he is making a defence."

palinode to 'The Lotos-Eaters,' " [33] though I think it is no such thing. It deals, of course, with an older Ulysses, a Ulysses who has restored Ithaca to order and intends "To sail beyond the sunset, and the baths / Of all the western stars" (60–61) until he dies. Of the poem, Tennyson said, " 'Ulysses' . . . was written soon after Arthur Hallam's death, and gave my feeling about the need of going forward, and braving the struggle of life perhaps more simply than anything in 'In Memoriam.' " [34] This statement does not commit us to a single interpretation of the poem, but it does turn Tennyson into a critic with whom we must deal.

The problem that has bothered critics is the difficulty of reconciling the opening lines of the poem—those which show Ulysses rejecting domestic responsibility and his responsibility to his nation and which evince a harsh attitude toward his people and a selfish individuality—with the closing lines which heroically express "the need of going forward, and braving the struggle of life." The poem has therefore been read by some, not as heroic, but as escapist, even suicidal. [35]

One can reconcile the opening and closing lines of the poem without resort to such a conclusion. One must, however, recognize that there are two kinds of death in the poem—a death suffered through the passive rejection of life and a death inevitable in the active acceptance of life. If the opening of the poem seems harsh, it seems so against the background of Tennyson's avowed acceptance of Victorian domesticity, his nationalism, and his love of order as evidenced in other poems. This poem, however, is not about those issues; it is about the acceptance of life through the acceptance of death.

33. Paull F. Baum, *Tennyson Sixty Years After* (Chapel Hill, N.C., 1948), p. 95. Cf. Marshall, *Handbook*, pp. 95–96.

34. *Memoir*, p. 163.

35. See, for example, Baum, p. 303; Joseph, pp. 28–29; E. J. Chiasson, "Tennyson's 'Ulysses'—A Reinterpretation," in *Critical Essays on the Poetry of Tennyson*, ed. John Killham (New York, 1967), p. 172; Steane, *Tennyson*, pp. 53–54; Ryals, *Theme and Symbol*, pp. 129, 130. Robert Langbaum, on the other hand, attributes to Ulysses a qualified choice of life: "Tennyson's Ulysses picks himself up from his Ithacan somnolence to make the choice for life; he will carry on, he will make the last effort, but with the same cry of pain that stirs Eliot's vegetable world in April, and with the same endurance of life only because it leads to death" (*The Poetry of Experience* [New York, 1963], p. 91).

More important than what the opening lines say is the way
they say it:

> It little profits that an idle king,
> By this still hearth, among these barren crags,
> Matched with an agèd wife, I mete and dole
> Unequal laws unto a savage race. . . .

As the diction suggests, such a life as that described is not life
but a kind of death: "Idle," "still," "barren," "Matched with an
agèd wife" all suggest the absence of action, fruition, change, purpose, and progress that are associated with life. It is this death-in-
life that Ulysses wishes to leave. Ulysses has done his work, has
restored Ithaca to order, and now turns the responsibilities of
kingship over to his son.[36] Telemachus has his work, but it is not
the work of Ulysses: Ulysses can do nothing about the still hearth
because he is old and "Matched with an agèd wife"; it is Telemachus who can produce the children who will prevent the hearth
from being still. Ulysses has fulfilled his paternal duties to Telemachus, whom he has loved (35), by providing him with his inheritance. If he speaks of his wife as "agèd," it is not to demean
her but to establish the fact that they are barren, like the crags,
and no longer have either youthful capacities or responsibilities
such as providing the kingdom with an heir, which at any rate they
have done.

Ulysses has as clear a recognition of the difference between
youth and age as has Rabbi Ben Ezra or the speaker of *Sailing to
Byzantium* or Tennyson's own ancient sage. He feels, however,
"How dull it is to pause, to make an end, / To rust unburnished,
not to shine in use! / As though to breathe were life" (22–24).
Merely to breathe is not life, but death-in-life; to choose merely
to breathe is to "make an end," to choose death. The "end"

---

36. King Arthur looks forward to the same end to duty in *The Holy Grail:*

> . . . the King must guard
> That which he rules, and is but as the hind
> To whom a space of land is given to plow,
> Who may not wander from the allotted field
> Before his work be done; but, being done,
> Let visions of the night or of the day
> Come, as they will. . . .   (901–7)

here spoken of, a passivity which is a kind of death, is opposed to the "end" of line 51: "Death closes all: but something ere the end, / Some work of noble note, may yet be done." Here the "end" is also death, but it is a different kind of death. It is a death which is met in the active pursuit of life, rather than a living death of passivity; it is also a death which is accepted but not "made" or chosen. It is not a death-in-life but a death which gives meaning to life. It is a death which makes life precious, which makes Ulysses think it vile to waste even three suns (28–29).

The opening and closing sections of *Ulysses* can therefore be reconciled if we see that the poem is about two kinds of death, one which must be rejected, the other which must be accepted though not sought. Read in this way, the beginning of the poem is a rejection, not of responsibility, but of passivity, and the end of the poem is an affirmation of active life in the face of death. The poem is therefore not suicidal, an "expression of a death wish," but an expression of a life wish, as it were. To accept the fact of death, as Ulysses does, is to make life meaningful. In 1833, faced with the fact of Hallam's death, Tennyson presumably had to accept that fact and go on. Ulysses, perhaps like Tennyson, hopes that "Some work of noble note, may yet be done" (52) before he is taken by death, but he has no fear of death. And though there is no certainty of immortality, there is at least the possibility of it: "It may be we shall touch the Happy Isles, / And see the great Achilles, whom we knew" (63–64). Death is accepted and life goes on, as Tennyson suggested in his comment on the poem.

Tithonus (1833, 1860) Tennyson described as "a pendent to the 'Ulysses,'" [37] and so it is. It is not "a pendent" because both express a death wish; [38] nor is it "a pendent" because *Tithonus* is antithetical to *Ulysses*,[39] as one seeks escape and the other involvement. It is "a pendent" because it is complementary to *Ulysses:* both are poems in which the protagonist accepts the fact of death, but both poems do not treat this acceptance in the same terms. On the contrary, it may be said that both poems come to

37. *Memoir,* p. 386.

38. See, for example, Ryals, *Theme and Symbol,* p. 130: " 'Tithonus' is much less ambiguous than 'Ulysses' in its statement of the death-wish."

39. See Johnson, *Alien Vision,* p. 41: *Ulysses* "is often taken as expressing a point of view directly contradictory to that embodied in *The Lotos-Eaters.* Actually the defeatism of *Tithonus* forms a more effective contrast."

the same conclusion from opposite directions. Metaphorically, Ulysses accepts death by his acceptance of the West. Tithonus accepts death by his rejection of the East.[40]

In both poems, the speakers reject a death-in-life: in *Ulysses* the "barren," "still," "idle" life in Ithaca; in *Tithonus* death is sought, but not "because life without term cannot give [Tithonus] a never-ending titillation of the senses,"[41] as one critic has suggested, and not because Tithonus is suicidal and a reflection of Tennyson's own suicidal tendencies.[42] Death is accepted as natural, indeed as providential. The "power to die" is a power given to "happy men" (70), for

> Why should a man desire in any way
> To vary from the kindly race of men,
> Or pass beyond the goal of ordinance
> Where all should pause, as is most meet for all?
>
> (28–31)

Death is the sensible and providential liberation of man from cruel immortality. *Tithonus* is therefore not a recommendation of suicide, but, on the contrary, a reconciliation to the fact of death through illustration of the cruelty of a world in which death is inoperative.

Such an acceptance of death is, of course, older than Christianity, but its Christian expression in no way implies that Christianity condones suicide. To take but one most obvious example: in Book X of *Paradise Lost* (1016–24), Adam clearly rejects as prideful and impious the suicide which Eve counsels. In Book XI (57–61) God as clearly states that death is a merciful gift from him to man:

> I at first with two fair gifts
> Created him endow'd, with Happiness
> And Immortality: that fondly lost,
> This other serv'd but to eternize woe;
> Till I provided Death. . . .

40. Cf. *Ulysses*, "for my purpose holds / To sail beyond the sunset, and the baths / Of all the western stars" (59–61), and *Tithonus*, "Yet hold me not for ever in thine East" (64). In an earlier version Tithonus asks to be lapped "within the lonely west." See Mary Joan Donahue, "Tennyson's 'Hail Briton!' and 'Tithon,'" *PMLA*, 64 (1949): 401, or Ricks, *Poems*, p. 567.

41. Chiasson, p. 172.

42. Marshall, *Handbook*, pp. 150–51.

TENNYSON
Some Early Poems

To accept death as a natural good, in other words, is not to condone suicide. Immortality is obviously not a gift to Tithonus but has become a punishment, as it is, for example, to the old man in *The Pardoner's Tale* or to the Struldbrugs. In all these cases death is not something cruel, but something benevolent. This does not mean that it should be sought by men, but it is sought by those who "vary from the kindly race of men," those who are condemned to an unnatural immortality.

It is suggested in the poem that Tithonus' immortality has become cruel, not as a result of the whim of arbitrary gods, but as the result of a kind of cosmic irony which, in granting Tithonus' wish, punishes him for his excessive pride. In seeking to vary from the kindly race of men, that is from his kind,[43] Tithonus is guilty of the same pride as the soul of *The Palace of Art* or the mariners of *The Lotos-Eaters*—"he seemed / To his great heart none other than a God!" (13–14). In seeking to be more than man, Tithonus has become less than man: he has lost the power to die. His immortality is not to be desired because it is unnatural and is contrasted in the poem to the immortality of Eos, which is natural. Eos, as the goddess of dawn, is a natural phenomenon and undergoes a daily rebirth. Birth, death, and rebirth, then, become the natural immortality as opposed to that of Tithonus. Eos can be reborn only because she dies. Death in the poem therefore becomes necessary to immortality, at least the only kind of immortality which should be wished for.

Far from being reflections of a Tennysonian death wish, both *Tithonus* and *Ulysses* are poems about man's reconciliation to the fact of death, written at a time in Tennyson's life when such a reconciliation was apparently imperative.[44] And contrary to the general critical comment on the poems, it seems to me that it is not *Ulysses* but *Tithonus* which is the study of pride. Read in this way, *Tithonus* is hardly escapist, but rather one of a number of early poems which concern themselves with the problem of pride, that pride which causes man to isolate himself from his fellow

43. The earlier version had "Why should a man desire in any shape / To vary from his kind"; see Donahue, p. 401, or Ricks, *Poems,* p. 567.

44. It should be noted, however, that the death of Hallam rather intensified than initiated Tennyson's interest in the problem of death. See such juvenilia, for example, as *Nothing Will Die, All Things Will Die, A Dirge, Love and Death,* and even a version of *The Two Voices;* see Ricks, *Poems,* p. 522.

men and lust after godhead. *St Simeon Stylites* (1833, 1842), a poem which has been generally neglected by critics and anthologists alike, is devoted to the same theme but in specifically Christian terms.

Simeon Stylites is a particularly apt subject for Tennyson because he has, like the soul in *The Palace of Art,* not only isolated himself from mankind, but has literally placed himself above mankind, first six cubits, then twelve, then twenty, and finally forty cubits high on his pillar. Where the soul in the palace enjoys "God-like isolation" from which she watches "the darkening droves of swine / That range on yonder plain," Simeon, in a similar isolation, "scarce can hear the people hum / About the column's base" (37–38). Although Simeon begins by asserting his kinship with mankind—"Although I be the basest of mankind, / From scalp to sole one slough and crust of sin" (1–2) [45]—it is a kinship in which he does not really believe, as he later refers to his "superhuman pangs" (11). Indeed, Simeon finds his kinship neither with common men nor with saints, as he is more saintly than the saints:

> O Jesus, if thou wilt not save my soul,
> Who may be saved? who is it may be saved?
> Who may be made a saint, if I fail here?
> Show me the man hath suffered more than I.
> For did not all thy martyrs die one death?
> For either they were stoned, or crucified,
> Or burned in fire, or boiled in oil, or sawn
> In twain beneath the ribs; but I die here
> Today, and whole years long, a life of death.
> (45–53)

Simeon, kin neither to men nor saints, finds his kinship ultimately with God, and even then perhaps not always in a subordinate position. In canonizing himself, Simeon necessarily deifies himself. Like the soul of *The Palace of Art,* he usurps God's prerogative by determining his own salvation: "It cannot be but that I shall be

---

45. In *The Palace of Art* mankind is described in similar language: "In filthy sloughs they roll a prurient skin, / They graze and wallow, breed and sleep" (201–2).

saved; / Yea, crowned a saint" (150–51), says Simeon.[46] He also attributes the power of working miracles to himself rather than to God through his agency:

> Yes, I can heal him. Power goes forth from me.
> They say that they are healed. Ah, hark! they shout
> 'St Simeon Stylites.' Why, if so,
> God reaps a harvest in me. O my soul,
> God reaps a harvest in thee. If this be,
> Can I work miracles and not be saved?
> This is not told of any. They were saints.   (143–49)

Finally, there is the interestingly ambiguous passage which seems to endow Simeon with godhead:

> It may be I have wrought some miracles,
> And cured some halt and maimed; but what of that?
> It may be, no one, even among the saints,
> May match his pains with mine; but what of that?
> Yet do not rise; for you may look on me,
> And in your looking you may kneel to God.   (134–39)

Though the passage may be read to mean that by honoring Simeon the people are also honoring God, it may also be read to mean that by kneeling to Simeon they are literally kneeling to God. "Am I to blame for this, / That here come those that worship me?" (122–23), Simeon asks. The answer, one suspects, is yes.

Though *St Simeon Stylites* may have been occasioned by the evangelicalism of Charles Simeon, a Fellow of King's College, Cambridge, as Jerome Buckley interestingly suggests,[47] and though it may reflect Tennyson's hostility to asceticism generally and the Calvinism of his Aunt Mary Bourne in particular, as many critics propose,[48] the poem deals also with themes which concerned

---

46. Of the soul in *The Palace of Art* Tennyson says, "Then of the moral instinct would she prate / And of the rising from the dead, / As hers by right of full-accomplished Fate . . ." (205–7).

47. *Tennyson*, p. 25.

48. See Sir Charles Tennyson, *Alfred Tennyson* (London, 1949), p. 194 (hereafter cited as *Tennyson*): "*St. Simeon Stylites* illustrates the morbid and vainglorious practice of asceticism—and I suspect that here there was a reference to the Calvinism of Aunt Mary Bourne." Also *Memoir*, p. 161: "As 'The Palace of

Tennyson again and again in the early poems. Although the pathological asceticism which delights in torments of the flesh is new, the determination of one's own salvation, the desire to be worshiped by men, the pride which attempts to differentiate or isolate itself from the rest of mankind—in general, the sublime egotism of such positions—and the theme of death-in-life, or as Simeon says "a life of death" (53), had interested Tennyson throughout the early years.

The burden of most of these early poems seems to be that a life of men and with men must be lived, and death, though not desired (as Simeon desires it, for example), must be accepted. The poems seem, at least to me, to insist that the impulse to isolation in man or poet reflects a pride which is stultifying to the soul and to the aesthetic sense, as man and poet are not separable entities nor are the moral and aesthetic sides of man's nature separable. Far from being destructive to the artist, therefore, the world of direct experience, of reality, of activity, of progress is imperative. If death ends life, it also makes life meaningful, and it is at any rate providential. The poems do not, I think, take a position which is escapist or defeatist, as has often been suggested. They express not negative but affirmative reactions to essential questions about art and life.

Art' represents the pride of voluptuous enjoyment in its noblest form, the 'St. Simeon Stylites' represents the pride of asceticism in its basest."

2. *In Memoriam:* A Prelude

*I*N MEMORIAM is certainly one of the great elegies in the English language, and of the great ones, it is the most perplexing. Even the briefest survey of critical opinion indicates the confusion which surrounds the poem. Early reviewers generally echoed Charles Kingsley's statement that *In Memoriam* was "the noblest English Christian poem which several centuries have seen."[1] Time, however, produced dissent from this view. T. S. Eliot was later to conclude of the poem, "Its faith is a poor thing, but its doubt is a very intense experience. *In Memoriam* is a poem of despair, but of despair of a religious kind."[2] Tennyson for one critic "had a good deal of the temperament of the mystic";[3] for another, he had "no sympathy with mystical religion."[4] For some, Tennyson is orthodox, for others heterodox. For all, *In Memoriam* is a poem of religious affirmation, but whether an affirmation of faith, of doubt, of despair, of Christianity, of quasi-Christian transcendentalism, or of what is not convincingly clarified.

The poem's meaning has not been the only obstacle in the path of a critical appreciation. Critics, disturbed by the apparent lack of unity in the poem, have suggested that there is a unity, but that it is externally arranged around the three Christmas sections, the anniversaries of Hallam's death, and the spring songs.[5]

1. Quoted in Edgar Finley Shannon, Jr., *Tennyson and the Reviewers* (Cambridge, Mass., 1952), p. 146.

2. "In Memoriam," in *Essays Ancient and Modern* (1936), reprinted in *Critical Essays on the Poetry of Tennyson,* p. 214.

3. T. S. Eliot, in *Critical Essays on the Poetry of Tennyson,* p. 212.

4. Baum, *Tennyson Sixty Years After,* p. 192.

5. Tennyson himself suggests such a structural division: "After the Death of A. H. H., the divisions of the poem are made by First Xmas Eve (Section

Others, encouraged by Tennyson's description of the poem as "the way of the soul," have found unity in autobiography—in the spiritual development of Tennyson himself from despair to faith [6] —or have seen a parallel aesthetic development and have described the movement of the poem as "The Way of the Poet." [7] Some have found the unity in the central fact of Hallam's death; [8] one has seen unity in the theme of change and has suggested that ultimately "it is the reader . . . who achieves the unity of the poem." [9] Many, of course, have given up trying to find the poem's unity,[10] accepting Tennyson's description of the lyrics as "short swallow flights of song," and maintain that unity is unnecessary to its greatness or that because it is not unified it fails of greatness.

These, then, are the two problems—the poem's meaning and the poem's unity—which a coherent critical appraisal must resolve if the integrity of the poem is to be established and understood. The first problem—what the poem is about—must necessarily be treated with the second problem—how the poem is unified—as the two problems are interdependent. As a matter of fact, one of the ways through which we know what the poem means is the form which the poem takes. Or, put another way, the subject of the

---

XXVIII.) , Second Xmas (Section LXXVIII.) , Third Xmas Eve (CIV. and CV. etc.) " (*Memoir*, p. 255) . Valerie Pitt makes a threefold division in the poem at the anniversary poems (LXXII and XCIX) rather than the traditional fourfold division at the Christmas poems, in *Tennyson Laureate* (Toronto, 1963) , p. 99. Robert Langbaum, though he accepts the three Christmases as "the most obvious markers of spiritual development," suggests a twofold division with "the real turning point" of the poem at section XCV—"The Dynamic Unity of *In Memoriam*," in *The Modern Spirit* (New York, 1970) , pp. 64, 65. See also Ricks' introduction to the poem (*Poems*, pp. 859–60) .

6. T. S. Eliot commented, ". . . *In Memoriam* is the whole poem. It is unique: it is a long poem made by putting together lyrics, which have only the unity and continuity of a diary, the concentrated diary of a man confessing himself. It is a diary of which we have to read every word" (*Critical Essays on the Poetry of Tennyson*, p. 212) .

7. E. D. H. Johnson, " 'In Memoriam': The Way of the Poet," *Victorian Studies*, 2 (1958) : 139–48.

8. See, for example, the reviewer in *Hogg's Instructor* (1850) : the poem is "thus made up of a series of detached parts, yet is the unity of the whole unbroken, because there is ever a recurrence to one and the same melancholy event" (quoted in Shannon, *Tennyson and the Reviewers*, p. 147) .

9. Jonathan Bishop, "The Unity of 'In Memoriam,' " *VN*, no. 21 (1962) : 13.

10. See Baum, *Tennyson Sixty Years After*, p. 115: ". . . we are not justified in looking for unity of tone or plan [in *In Memoriam*]."

poem both determines and is reflected in its form. The poem's unity is, in the Coleridgean sense, organic.

First, the poem's meaning: *In Memoriam* is not, I think, finally about Arthur Hallam; in the poem, he is a means rather than an end. Nor is *In Memoriam,* except incidentally, a poem of despair. It is, rather, a poem about the unity behind the diversity and change of the cosmic process. Both Hallam and the feelings of the persona subserve the central concern of the poem, which is with the manifestation of the spiritual unity in the diversity of the natural world. That is, the subject of the poem is the one-ness that manifests itself as multiplicity, and that subject is discovered to us through the developing perception of the persona.

Second, the poem's unity: The unity of the poem, that is, its aesthetic wholeness, as well as the relation of the parts to the whole, is both a formal and a structural one. In other words, the poem has an internal unity of form, an organic unity if you will, which is different from the external structural unity usually attributed to it, the structural unity of four parts divided by the three Christmases. The formal unity is the unity of a process rather than the structural unity of a thing. Or, put figuratively, the one-ness of the poem is like the oneness of a river moving inevitably toward the sea, as differentiated from the oneness of a structure like a building. *In Memoriam* finds its unity in the consistent vision of the persona as he progresses from a perception of the "cosmic process" to a perception of the spiritual unity behind that cosmic process, in which progress he follows an artistically controlled course. In the Coleridgean sense, then, the unity of form in *In Memoriam* lies in its imitation of the process by which the persona progresses in spiritual awareness.

In order both to clarify and to give evidence for these assertions, I must indulge in a considerable prelude to my examination of the poem itself. First, the sense in which the poem is about the spiritual unity behind the diversity of the phenomenal world can best be illustrated against the background of Liberal Anglican theological thinking and of Tennyson's knowledge of such thought. Second, in order to demonstrate the artistic control which Tennyson exercised in unifying his material, I must distinguish between the persona of the poem and the poet, and between the Hallam of the poem and the real Arthur Hallam. I can then illustrate by examination of the poem itself. To begin with, the Liberal Anglican background.

*

"The theology of [*In Memoriam*]," it has been said, "was from Rugby: it is the voice of the Broad Church. . . ." [11] Though there is some truth in such an assertion, that truth is complex; the "theology" of *In Memoriam* reflects that of a movement rather than that of a party and therefore should perhaps be identified with Liberal Anglicanism rather than the Broad Church. [12] And, of course, the "theology" does not come directly from Rugby. Thomas Arnold, famous headmaster of Rugby, was a great force in the Liberal Anglican movement of the early nineteenth century, but his was neither the only voice nor the most directly influential one for Tennyson; equally vocal were Connop Thirlwall, Henry Hart Milman, Arthur Stanley, Julius Hare, and F. D. Maurice. Of these, it was the last two—Hare and Maurice—who most directly affected Tennyson.

Julius Hare was resident Fellow of Trinity College, Cambridge, during Tennyson's stay there and attracted the discipleship of John Sterling, the leader of the Apostles, of whom he wrote a biography. Of his time at Cambridge, Tennyson said, "The German School, with Coleridge, Julius Hare, etc. to expound, came to reform all our notions." [13] Maurice, later to become Hare's brother-in-law, was generally regarded as the spiritual founder of the Apostles, and though he left Trinity and Cambridge in 1827, the year in which Tennyson matriculated, his in-

11. Joseph Jacobs, *Tennyson & In Memoriam* (London, 1892), p. 10; also, "*In Memoriam* has liberalised theology, and been to the Broad Church movement what *The Christian Year* has been to the High Church" (p. 18).

12. I am seeking to avoid a confusion here. Duncan Forbes, for example, uses the term "Broad Church" as a party label attached to a single faction of the Liberal Anglican movement in its degeneration; see *The Liberal Anglican Idea of History* (Cambridge, 1952), p. 118. F. D. Maurice also strongly objected to the label "Broad Church" late in life, though in the twenties and thirties he was associated with the Liberal Anglican movement. See Maurice's introductory essay to Julius Hare's *Victory of Faith*, ed. E. H. Plumptre (London, 1874), pp. xvii–lxxxix.

13. *Memoir*, p. 30. Jacobs says, "The influence of Coleridge was transmitted to Tennyson through John Sterling and Frederick Denison Maurice" (*Tennyson & In Memoriam*, p. 100).

fluence was pervasive. In a letter to Gladstone, Arthur Hallam said of Maurice, "The effect which he has produced on the minds of many at Cambridge by the single creation of that society of 'Apostles' (for the spirit though not the form was created by him) is far greater than I can dare to calculate, and will be felt, both directly and indirectly, in the age that is upon us." [14] Maurice was, of course, later to become a close friend of Tennyson and to dedicate his *Theological Essays* to the poet. The thought of both men was clearly accessible to Tennyson from 1827 on and so probably was that of their fellow Liberal Anglicans. [15]

The Liberal Anglicans were a rather heterogeneous group of men. [16] But they were all historians, as well as theologians, and expounded a developmental theory of history, which they derived indirectly from Niebuhr and directly from Giambattista Vico's *Scienza Nuova*. [17] In that theory there are two kinds of

14. *Memoir,* p. 36.

15. Tennyson apparently never met Dr. Arnold, nor was his friendship with Arnold's biographer, Dean Stanley, initiated until some time later (see *Memoir,* p. 612). Sir Charles Tennyson suggests that Tennyson met Henry Hart Milman for the first time in 1865 (*Tennyson,* p. 359), though Tennyson may have read Milman's *History of the Jews* (1829), while at Cambridge. Connop Thirlwall, on the other hand, was a resident fellow at Cambridge and a defender of the "Apostles" during Tennyson's tenure there: see Mrs. Charles Brookfield, *The Cambridge Apostles* (New York, 1906), p. 13. See also Sir Charles Tennyson, *Tennyson,* pp. 68–70.

16. Maurice, for example, really belongs on the fringe of this group. He is not one of the six Liberal Anglicans of the "Germano-Coleridgean school" examined in detail by Forbes in *The Liberal Anglican Idea of History.* He is, however, grouped with Hare and Arnold by Charles Richard Sanders in *Coleridge and the Broad Church Movement* (Durham, N.C., 1942). See also Plumptre's comment, "Hare, Maurice, Stanley, and Thirlwall . . . these are, I suppose, classed together in popular estimate, if not as the leaders of a party, at least as the representatives of a school" ("Preface" to Hare's *Victory of Faith,* p. xiv). Robert Preyer includes among the "Germano-Coleridgeans" Hare, Thirlwall, Arnold, Milman, Whatley, Goldwin Smith, Stanley, Sterling, and Maurice: *Bentham, Coleridge, and the Science of History,* Beiträge zur Englischen Philologie, no. 41 (1958), pp. 88–90.

17. Forbes, *The Liberal Anglican Idea of History,* p. 39. Tennyson's familiarity with Niebuhr and the "Germano-Coleridgean school" is indisputable. Niebuhr, we are told by Mrs. Brookfield, for the Apostles "was a god, who for a lengthy period formed all their sentiments" (*The Cambridge Apostles,* p. 8). Niebuhr was, of course, of the "German School" expounded by Hare, which Tennyson alludes to in the *Memoir* (p. 30); Hare and Connop Thirlwall translated the first two volumes of Niebuhr's *History of Rome* while at Cambridge. Niebuhr's *History* was also among the books later lent by Tennyson's wife to a friend; see Sir Charles Tennyson, *Tennyson,* p. 282.

progress: the cyclical progress of national history, which can be studied scientifically as a natural phenomenon, and the "true progress" of universal history, which can be subjected to philosophical scrutiny. True progress is neither cyclical nor natural but rather linear and spiritual. As Duncan Forbes points out:

If [for the Liberal Anglicans] . . . history is fundamentally rhythmical, and the fact of progress plain to Christian eyes, the pattern of universal history must be a series of forward steps, each cycle of national history representing, so far as true progress is concerned, an advance on its predecessor, and this must be God's plan in the unfolding of his purpose. True progress, then, is a gradual advance, through the childhood-manhood rhythm of nations, towards the final goal of God's purpose which it is not given us to see. Progress is a perfection of the things of the spirit, and "progress" can only be cyclical on the lower plane, where maturity passes over into a new barbarism. In so far as a period is in advance of its predecessor, it is so where the things of the spirit are concerned, for here alone is true progress. As Christianity represents the highest point of progress so far attained, it is only a Christian philosophy of history, that is, universal history from a Christian point of view, which will reveal true progress.[18]

For the Liberal Anglicans, the progress of nations and the progress of individuals were very closely analogous, and it is for this reason that the primary metaphor used to describe the growth of nations for Hare and Arnold and Stanley was the life cycle of the individual. Perhaps the use of the metaphor and the relationship between the individual and the nation can best be illustrated by a quotation from Hare's *Guesses at Truth: Second Series:* "The natural life of nations, as well as of individuals, has its fixed course and term. It springs forth, grows up, reaches its maturity, decays, perishes. Only through Christianity has a nation ever risen again: and it is solely on the operation of Christianity that we can ground anything like a reasonable hope of the perfectibility of mankind; a hope that what has often been wrought in individuals, may also in the fulness of time be wrought by the same power in the race."[19]

18. Forbes, *The Liberal Anglican Idea of History*, pp. 65–66; see also p. 101.

19. (London, n.d.; Two Series in One Volume), pp. 248–49. The second series was originally published in 1848; both series were published under the authorship of "Two Brothers" (Augustus J. and Julius C. Hare).

Clearly Hare makes a distinction between the natural progress of nations and the potential spiritual progress of individuals and of the race. As I have said, true progress was for the Liberal Anglicans spiritual, and so it was for Tennyson.[20] But a belief in such progress necessitated a developmental theory of history.

It is such a theory of history which allows the persona to speak of the "one far-off divine event, / To which the whole creation moves" in the epithalamium of *In Memoriam,* that is, a developmental theory which can allow spiritual progress. It is such a theory behind the conception of Hallam as a type or prefiguration of man in spiritual advance of present men.[21] It is such a theory which lies behind the persona's exhortation to "Ring in the Christ that is to be" in section CVI, an exhortation apparently grounded in an acceptance of progressive revelation. It is finally such a theory which is the means for reconciling the change and diversity of nature with the permanence and unity of God.

This brings us to a second consideration: the relationship be-

20. Cf. Eugene R. August: "[T. S.] Eliot . . . failed to distinguish between the Philistine 'doctrine' of materialistic progress which Tennyson opposed and the 'doctrine' of spiritual progress that he accepted and praised"; and "Tennyson and Teilhard mean much the same thing by progress, namely spiritual growth . . ." ("Tennyson and Teilhard: The Faith of *In Memoriam,*" *PMLA,* 84 [1969]: 223, 221). In this most illuminating article, Professor August not only examines very cogently the nature of Tennyson's faith, but demonstrates its modernity.

21. It may be true, as Mrs. Mattes suggests, that Tennyson "was almost certainly indebted to Chambers [his *Vestiges of Creation,* 1844] for the following suggestion that Hallam's rare gifts and virtues had a special relation to the greater man of the future: 'Whereof the man, that with me trod / This planet, was a noble type / Appearing ere the times were ripe' (Epi. 137–139). For Chambers predicted that the '*nobler type* of humanity' he anticipated would 'realize some of the dreams of the purest spirits of the present race' " (Eleanor Bustin Mattes, *In Memoriam: The Way of a Soul* [New York, 1951], p. 85). But it would be a mistake to see Hallam as merely a biological sport of some kind, as a physical and intellectual improvement on the present race of men. Chambers apparently anticipates a nobler kind of man; Tennyson may see Hallam as a nobler kind of man, but we are also justified, I think, in understanding the word *type* in its theological sense of prefiguration. Hallam, in other words, prefigures man in advance of present men. As Adam, the living soul, was a type of Christ, the quickening spirit, that is, he prefigured Christ, so perhaps is Hallam a type of the coming spiritual man. Tennyson apparently uses the word *type* in its theological sense in other places, e.g., in section CXVIII of *In Memoriam* and in part VII, l. 281 of *The Princess.* John Killham understands this second example as biological; see *Tennyson and "The Princess"* (London, 1958), p. 261n. See also Elton Edward Smith, *The Two Voices* (Lincoln, Neb., 1964), pp. 110, 141, for the possible meanings of *type* in *In Memoriam.*

tween permanence and change and the consequent relationship between unity and diversity. If the Liberal Anglicans insisted on the necessity for change in the natural world, they were no less insistent on the permanence of God in the spiritual world. They reconciled the natural world with the spiritual world by the principle of accommodation, which "became the key-point of the Liberal Anglican philosophy of history." [22] God, for the Liberal Anglicans (though the principle is as old as Christianity), accommodates himself to man at every stage of man's historical development. God does not change, but the revelation of God adapts itself to man's capacity to apprehend that revelation. As Julius Hare puts it: "If we look at [Christianity] historically, it is at once unchangeable and changeable, at once constant and progressive. Were it not unchangeable and constant, it could not be the manifestation of Him who is the same yesterday, to-day, and for ever. Were it not changeable and progressive, it would not be suited to him with whom to-day is never like yesterday, nor to-morrow like to-day. Therefore it is both at once; one in its essence and changeless, as coming from God; manifold and variable in its workings, as designed to pervade and hallow every phase and element of man's being, his thoughts, his words, his deeds, his imagination, his reason, his affections, his duties." [23]

God, who is constant but manifests himself in progress, who is unchanging but manifests himself through change, is also unity who manifests himself as diversity. Hare describes the diversity which the phenomenal world imposes upon unity with a Shelleyan

22. Forbes, *The Liberal Anglican Idea of History*, p. 64.

23. *Guesses at Truth: Second Series*, p. 250. See also p. 251: "In this manner Christianity also becomes subject to the law of change, to which Time and all its births bow down. In a certain sense too the change is a progress; that is to say, in extent. Christianity is ever conquering some new province of human nature, some fresh national variety of mankind, some hitherto untenanted unexplored region of thought or feeling." Cf. Dean Stanley: "The everlasting mountains are everlasting, not because they are unchanged, but because they go on changing their form, their substance with the wear and tear of ages. 'The Everlasting Gospel' is everlasting, not because it remains stationary, but because, being the same, it can adapt itself to the constant change of society, of civilization, of humanity itself" (quoted in Forbes, *The Liberal Anglican Idea of History*, p. 75). Cf. Tennyson's conviction "that the forms of Christian religion would alter; but that the spirit of Christ would still grow from more to more 'in the roll of the ages.'. . . This was one of my meanings [he said] of 'Ring in the Christ that is to be'" (*Memoir*, p. 273).

metaphor when he speaks of ideas "brought down into the region of the empirical understanding, and contemplated under the relations of time and space": he says of every idea, "being one and simple in its own primordial fulness, it splits, when it enters into the prismatic atmosphere of human nature." [24] Hare clarifies the relationship between the idea and its manifestation, between God's unity and the diversity of the world, in his sermon on "The Unity of the Church":

> The desire of unity is inherent in man. It pervades all the expressions, all the modifications of his being, and may in a manner be termed an elementary principle of his nature. It lies, very often without his being conscious of it, at the bottom of all the workings of his mind, which is ever seeking, in one way or other, to infuse unity into the objects of its contemplation, to bring them under one head, to arrange them under one law, to find out some analogy, some relation, some likeness and harmony amongst them. . . .
>
> That this desire of beholding unity in all things arises from that unity of consciousness, in which man was made, and in which his Maker mirrored His own unity, cannot well be doubted. But while we have this principle of unity within us, we are set in the midst of a world, in which everything, when we first look out over it, seems to jar and war against all unity, a world which at first sight may seem to be just emerging or subsiding out of Chaos. The character of the outward world as it presents itself to our senses, is not unity, but multitude. It rushes upon us wave after wave, with a confused noise of many waters, entering into our minds by every inlet, taking possession of us, and almost overwhelming us. Its name is Legion. . . .
>
> The principle, I said, which leads and compels us to seek for unity in all the objects of our contemplation, notwithstanding the diversity and multiplicity and contrariety wherewith they assail us, is the unity of our consciousness, in which our Divine Maker mirrored the unity of His own being. . . . That there must be an essential unity pervading all God's works, is implied indeed in the very fact of their being His works. . . . There [must] be a unity running through

24. *Guesses at Truth: Second Series,* p. 250. Cf. Sanders on Coleridge: "All power manifested itself 'in the harmony of correspondent Opposites, each supposing and supporting the other,' and opposite powers were always of the same kind and tended to union, 'either by equipose or by a common product' " (*Coleridge and the Broad Church Movement,* p. 26). Tennyson uses the same prismatic metaphor as Hare in the Prologue to *In Memoriam,* in *Will Waterproof's Lyrical Monologue,* and in *The Higher Pantheism.*

all the works of Him who is essentially and entirely and indivisibly and eternally One. But this unity we cannot make out, unless we gain sight of its principle, unless we have hold of the only clue with the aid of which we can explore the multitudinous chambers in the endless labyrinth of the universe,—unless we can trace back the countless streams of life to their one primary source in the Wisdom and Goodness of their Author.[25]

For Hare, then, and for Maurice as well,[26] the diversity of the world is the providential manifestation of its essential unity.[27] For Tennyson the same thing is true.

We are told by Hallam Tennyson that his father "conceived that the further science progressed, the more the Unity of Nature, and the purpose hidden behind the cosmic process of matter in motion and changing forms of life, would be apparent."[28] That the unity of nature as well as the purpose behind the cosmic process is spiritual, that the natural world is a manifestation of the spiritual, is suggested by a further quotation from the *Memoir*: Hallam Tennyson tells us that his father was "inclined to think that the theory of Evolution caused the world to regard more clearly the 'Life of Nature as a lower stage in the manifestation of a principle which is more fully manifested in the spiritual life of man, with the idea that in this process of Evolution the lower is to be regarded as a means to the higher.'"[29] Tennyson seems clearly to be defending here both the validity and the value of Evolution; moreover, he seems to suggest that the natural world, rightly understood, is our means to spiritual advancement, that is, that natural knowledge can lead to spiritual wisdom.

I suggest that it is precisely this belief that is the burden of *In Memoriam*. The spiritual progress of the persona, his develop-

---

25. *The Mission of the Comforter* (London, 1846) , 1:263–65.

26. For Maurice's "leading idea of unity in diversity within the Kingdom of Christ," see Basil Willey, *More Nineteenth Century Studies* (New York, 1966) , p. 62.

27. For the Liberal Anglican distinction between unity and uniformity, see Forbes, *The Liberal Anglican Idea of History*, p. 85, and Hare's dedication to Henry Edward Manning of his Sermon "The Unity of the Church," in *The Mission of the Comforter*, 1:215–62.

28. *Memoir*, p. 270. Cf. lines 191–94 of *The Ancient Sage:* "But that one ripple on the boundless deep / Feels that the deep is boundless, and itself / For ever changing form, but evermore / One with the boundless motion of the deep."

29. *Memoir*, p. 271.

ment from knowledge to wisdom, is reflected in his changing perception of the world. Where at the beginning he had seen only chaos, at the end he sees cosmos; where there had once been only change, there is now permanence; where all had been diversity, there is unity. Change and diversity continue to exist, of course, in the natural world, but they are seen through wisdom to be manifestations of permanence and unity. Moreover, the persona undergoes a changing perception of Arthur Hallam, who is a natural manifestation of and a means to the spiritual world of permanence and unity, and that world is a Christian one. As we shall see, it is the persona's love for Hallam which leads him to a love for Christ, and it is his love for and trust in Christ which allows him to see the unity in Christ behind "the cosmic process of matter in motion and changing forms of life." [30]

*

In order to demonstrate that Hallam is at once the friend of Tennyson and an artistic creation, a vehicle for the persona's spiritual advancement, it is necessary to question the generally held assumption that *In Memoriam* is personally, fundamentally, and finally about Arthur Hallam and Tennyson's grief over his death. [31] It is imperative, it seems to me, to distinguish the persona of the poem from the real Tennyson and to distinguish the friend from the real Hallam.

Because *In Memoriam* is so often read autobiographically, it is necessary at least to reconsider whether Tennyson's grief over

30. I agree with Professor August on the nature of the Christ which Tennyson conceived. In comparing Tennyson with Teilhard, he says, "Both *In Memoriam* and *The Phenomenon of Man* are concerned with a faith beyond the forms of faith. Neither work seems overtly permeated by Christianity, but both are (in the authors' opinions) valid developments of it. Both men believe in a cosmic Christianity and a Christ beyond the merely sectarian Christs." And later, "The Prologue to *In Memoriam,* written last, is the most openly Christian part of the poem, yet it too shies away from sectarian Christianity and points instead to a Christ who is both personal and cosmic" ("Tennyson and Teilhard," p. 223).

31. See, for example, John D. Rosenberg, "The Two Kingdoms of *In Memoriam,*" *JEGP,* 58 (1959): 232: "For Hallam when alive was very nearly the center of Tennyson's life, and Hallam dead was the focal point of his life during the poem's composition. Despite its overlay of conventional pastoral elegy, *In Memoriam* is deeply, in places almost obnoxiously, personal."

Hallam's death has not been exaggerated.[32] Of course, Tennyson was more deeply affected by the death of Hallam than Shelley was by that of Keats or Milton by that of King, but the reader who concentrates on the personal in the poem often blinds himself to the universal. To begin with, those poems of reconciliation to death—*Ulysses, Tithonus,* and *Morte d'Arthur*—were written within a few months of Hallam's death,[33] and to project a deep grief over the years seems to me to ignore such evidence. Second, an examination of some early sections of *In Memoriam,* early in terms of placement in the poem and early perhaps in terms of composition, suggests that the poet controls the persona. In other words, Tennyson, at least by the time he came to arrange the individual sections, was the artist in control of his material, not the man controlled by his grief.

The distinction between the poet and the persona in the poem can be illustrated by the distinction between their perceptions. Section XII is the fourth of the "ship stanzas,"[34] those that deal with the ship that brings Hallam's body back to England:

32. See Ralph Wilson Rader, *Tennyson's* Maud: *The Biographical Genesis* (Berkeley, 1963), p. 11: "*In Memoriam,* first· of all, has made it easy to imagine Tennyson's life in the years after 1833 as completely dominated by the fact of the death—as an uneventful and homogeneous expanse of slowly lightening sorrow extending indefinitely toward the 1840's and ending, temporarily at least, with the poet's engagement to Emily Sellwood. The loose, chronologically vague account in the *Memoir,* together with a notable absence of documents from the period, has made such a notion easy to sustain. Sir Charles Tennyson's biography, however, has now sharpened and integrated our conception of this period and filled it out with new materials, so that an uncomplicated view of it is no longer possible. But even yet, because the documentary record is still so sparse, we assign perhaps too decisive an influence to Hallam's death. . . ." Mary Joan Ellmann comes to the same conclusion in "Tennyson: Unpublished Letters, 1833–36," *MLN,* 65 (1950) : 223–28.

33. See *Memoir,* pp. 163, 92. *Tithonus,* first published in *Cornhill* in 1860, was written before the end of 1833; *Ulysses* is dated in J. M. Heath's Commonplace Book October 20, 1833, twenty days after Tennyson heard of Hallam's death. See Marshall, *Handbook,* p. 95.

34. The first of the "ship stanzas," section IX, beginning "Fair ship," is the earliest written section of the poem (1833). Section XII may have been written around the same time, as it employs the image of the body as mortal ark, an image used by Tennyson in *The Two Voices* (l. 389), written in 1833; see *Memoir,* p. 92. There is convincing evidence for a later date, however. Section XII does not appear in the Trinity MSS but does appear in the Lincoln Library MS, dated 1842. Ricks suggests that the new sections in the Lincoln Library MS were probably written between 1837 and 1845–46 (*Poems,* p. 858) .

> Lo, as a dove when up she springs
>   To bear through Heaven a tale of woe,
>   Some dolorous message knit below
> The wild pulsation of her wings;
>
> Like her I go; I cannot stay;
>   I leave this mortal ark behind,
>   A weight of nerves without a mind,
> And leave the cliffs, and haste away
>
> O'er ocean-mirrors rounded large,
>   And reach the glow of southern skies,
>   And see the sails at distance rise,
> And linger weeping on the marge,
>
> And saying; 'Comes he thus, my friend?
>   Is this the end of all my care?'
>   And circle moaning in the air:
> 'Is this the end? Is this the end?'

The fourth quatrain ends in a question, but the poet answers the question for us through his use of the dominant images of the dove and the ark. The juxtaposition of the two objects suggests the context which makes them most meaningful. Noah's question, when he sends the dove from the ark, is essentially, "Is this the end? Is this the end?" The return of the dove from the second trip with the olive branch and its failure to return from the third trip confirm for Noah that this is not the end.[35] My point is that by section XII where the persona questions, the poet not only sees clearly the answer but suggests it through the imagery—no, this is not the end. The indication is that the poet knew very early in the poem as we now have it what direction the persona would take.

An even earlier section also suggests that the poet sees, and hopefully the reader will see, the pattern which the poem will follow. Section VII, the section in which the persona first goes to Hallam's house, ends with the following quatrain:

---

35. The dove, both in the poem and traditionally, is a symbol of the spirit. Tennyson's drawing our attention to the mortality of the ark may differentiate it from the spirit, which is immortal. At any rate, in the poem, it is through the spirit that the persona comes to recognize that this is not the end.

> He is not here; but far away
>   The noise of life begins again,
>   And ghastly through the drizzling rain
> On the bald street breaks the blank day.

The persona sees nothing but the house of Hallam; the poet, however, associates the house with the tomb of Christ. In three of
the four gospels, the phrase "He is not here" appears when Christ's
tomb is found empty: [36] "He is not here: for he is risen" (Matt.
28:6) ; "he is risen; he is not here" (Mark 16:6) ; "He is not here,
but is risen" (Luke 24:6) . By associating the house with Christ's
tomb, the poet suggests hope where the persona finds none. By
repeating the gospel phrase, Tennyson is perhaps suggesting at
once that Hallam has risen and that we are to associate Hallam
with Christ. Indeed, as we shall see, an examination of the pattern
of the imagery and the development of the central symbol in the
poem bears out such a suggestion.

If it is true then that we must not confuse the persona of the
poem with the poet, it is equally true that we must not confuse
the Hallam of the poem with the real Hallam. I do not, of course,
wish to deny that very real feelings were generated in Tennyson
by his friend's death. I mean only to suggest that the real Tennyson and the real Hallam are transformed in the poem into the
material of a work of art. In this regard it is perhaps helpful to
see the relation between *In Memoriam* and the literary genre of
the confession, where similar kinds of transformations take place.
Commentators on *In Memoriam* have noted similarities between
it and Augustine's *Confessions* and *Sartor Resartus*,[37] but it can
perhaps be compared more specifically and profitably to Dante's
Vita Nuova.

36. I am indebted to Mrs. Opal Kaney for first pointing out this correspondence to me, though I later discovered that Rosenberg ("The Two Kingdoms
of *In Memoriam*," p. 230) had made the same identification. He even describes
the house as "itself an image of the tomb" of Christ, though he does not identify
Hallam himself with Christ, nor does he distinguish between poet and persona.

37. A. C. Bradley, in *A Commentary on Tennyson's* In Memoriam (London,
1910) , illustrates *In Memoriam* four times with the *Confessions*—pp. 87, 90, 106,
178; Archibald MacMechan, in the introduction to his edition of *Sartor Resartus*
(Boston, 1896) , suggests specific verbal echoes of *Sartor Resartus* in *In Memoriam*,
p. lxx*n*.

We are told in the *Memoir* that in 1830 Tennyson "took great interest in the work which Hallam had undertaken, a translation from the *Vita Nuova* of Dante, with notes and prefaces." [38] It is not unreasonable to assume that, in writing an elegy for Hallam, Tennyson may have had in mind the poet Hallam particularly favored. I do not mean, of course, that because *In Memoriam* can be associated with confessional literature it is therefore merely autobiographical. It is no more merely autobiographical than the *Vita Nuova;* it should no more be reduced to Tennyson's grief over the death of Hallam than the *Vita Nuova* or its "natural prolongation," [39] the *Divine Comedy,* can be reduced to Dante's grief over the death of Beatrice. In other words, as the real Beatrice Portinari is transformed by the artist Dante, so in a like manner is the real Hallam transformed by the artist Tennyson. [40]

Here it may be helpful to identify certain specific correspondences between *In Memoriam* and the *Vita Nuova* in order to see how autobiographical material can and should be generalized in a work of art. Beatrice, in the *Vita Nuova,* is transformed into Christ. Dante suggests this when he associates Giovanna, the woman who precedes Beatrice while they walk, with John, "since her name Giovanna is derived from that Giovanni (John) who preceded the true light, saying, '*Ego vox clamantis in deserto, Parate viam Domini.*'" [41] Hallam himself saw Beatrice in essentially this light: of the *Divine Comedy,* that extension of the *Vita Nuova,* he says, "In the 'Paradise,' and the latter part of the 'Purgatory,' we have intimated already, that the reality of Beatrice Portinari seemed, for a time, to become absorbed into those

38. P. 37. At this time, Hallam wrote to Tennyson: "I expect to glean a good deal of knowledge from you concerning metres which may be serviceable, as well for my philosophy in the notes as for my actual handiwork in the text. I purpose to discuss considerably about poetry in general, and about the ethical character of Dante's poetry" (*Memoir,* p. 38). For Aubrey De Vere's comment on the analogy between *In Memoriam* and *The Divine Comedy,* see *Memoir,* p. 245.

39. The words are Hallam's: "On Gabriele Rossetti's Dante Theories," in *The Writings of Arthur Hallam,* ed. T. H. Vail Motter (New York, 1943), p. 256 (hereafter cited as *Hallam*). In an article which appeared after this book was finished, Gordon D. Hirsch argues also for Tennyson's indebtedness to the *Vita Nuova* and the *Divine Comedy.* See "Tennyson's *Commedia,*" *VP,* 8 (1970) : 93–106.

40. Hallam energetically defends the reality of Beatrice Portinari against Rossetti's assertion that she did not exist; see "On Gabriele Rossetti's Dante Theories," *Hallam,* pp. 237–79.

41. *Vita Nuova,* trans. Theodore Martin (London, 1862), p. 45.

celestial truths, of which she had always been a mirror to the imagination of her lover. Described throughout as most pure, most humble, most simple, most affectionate, and as the personal form in which Dante delighted to contemplate the ideal objects of his moral feelings, is it wonderful that she should become at last for him the representative of religion itself?" [42]

In *In Memoriam*, I suggest, Hallam plays the same role that Beatrice plays for Dante. Hallam, too, is transformed into Christ; he becomes "absorbed into those celestial truths," becomes "the personal form" through which the poet contemplates "the ideal objects of his moral feelings." The spiritual advance of the persona, effected by his love for Hallam, allows him to accept this transformation. The fusion of Hallam and Christ is no more than Hallam himself expected of all Christians: "the tendency of love is towards a union so intimate, as virtually to amount to identification; when then by affection towards Christ we have become blended with his being, the beams of Eternal Love falling, as ever, on the one beloved object will include us in him, and their returning flashes of love out of his personality will carry along with them some from our own, since ours has become confused with his, and so shall we be one with Christ and through Christ with God." [43]

The principle of spiritual advancement in *In Memoriam* is love, as it had been for Dante, Spenser, and Milton. Human love can lead to divine love, is indeed apparently the only path to divine love. As F. D. Maurice said in *The Kingdom of Christ* (1838), "Human relationships are not artificial types of something divine, but are actually the means, and the only means through which man ascends to any knowledge of the divine." [44] It is perhaps in this sense that Tennyson meant that "in this process of Evolution the lower [life of nature] is to be regarded as a means to the higher [life of spirit]." [45] At any rate, what Hal-

42. "On Gabriele Rossetti's Dante Theories," *Hallam,* pp. 256–57. To suggest an analogy between the *Divine Comedy* and *In Memoriam* is to do no more than Tennyson himself did when he remarked that *In Memoriam* "was meant to be a kind of *Divina Commedia,* ending with happiness" (*Memoir,* p. 255).

43. "Theodicaea Novissima," *Hallam,* p. 210.

44. Quoted in W. Merlin Davies, *An Introduction to F. D. Maurice's Theology* (London, 1964), p. v.

45. *Memoir,* p. 271.

lam says of *The Divine Comedy* applies also to *In Memoriam:* "But it was not in scattered sonnets that the whole magnificence of that idea could be manifested, which represents love as at once the base and pyramidal point of the entire universe, and teaches us to regard the earthly union of souls, not as a thing accidental, transitory, and dependent on the condition of human society, but with far higher import, as the best and the appointed symbol of our relations with God, and through them of his own ineffable essence." [46]

The love between Tennyson and Hallam should be seen in the poem similarly "as the best and appointed symbol of our relations with God." It has been the failure to see the love as symbolic which has led critics to be made uncomfortable by what an early reviewer called "the tone of . . . amatory tenderness" [47] and a later critic has described as "the exceptionally close male relationship of a pre-Freudian age." [48] Because Tennyson sees the love as symbolic, he can describe the persona as "widowed" by the loss of Hallam just as Dante had described the world as "widowed" by the loss of Beatrice or as Hofrath Heuschrecke finds his heart "widowed" by the loss of Teufelsdröckh. Tennyson seems to me to be simply working within the tradition which sees all humans as feminine in their relation to God, a tradition certainly familiar to Donne, for example, and to Dante.[49]

To establish more clearly the role which Hallam plays in *In Memoriam*, I will now turn to my examination of the poem itself.

46. "The Influence of Italian upon English Literature," *Hallam*, pp. 224–25.

47. See Shannon, *Tennyson and the Reviewers*, pp. 156, 220*n*45.

48. Smith, *The Two Voices*, p. 83.

49. See Donne's "Holy Sonnet xiv," for example, and Charles Williams' comment, "And because all humans are, in [a] sense, feminine to God, therefore Dante can properly use the phrases of Saint Mary of himself" (*The Figure of Beatrice* [London, 1958], p. 61) .

3. *In Memoriam:* The Poem

*A*FTER a rather lengthy preliminary, it is time to turn to *In Memoriam* itself. In my examination of the poem I hope to establish three things. First, I hope to show that the poem is a work of art rather than conventional autobiography by demonstrating how Hallam serves his artistic function in the work. I wish to show, second, that the formal unity of the poem is achieved by the poet's concentration on the persona's change from

> . . . that delirious man
> Whose fancy fuses old and new,
> And flashes into false and true,
> And mingles all without a plan   (XVI)

into a man who sees

> . . . in part
> That all, as in some piece of art,
> Is toil cöoperant to an end.   (CXXVIII)

and that this change is mirrored in the change of image patterns in the poem; the change in image patterns is not, however, the replacement of one image by another (the replacement of darkness by light, for example) as is usually suggested,[1] but rather a gradual fusion of apparently antithetical images. And, third, I wish to demonstrate that the structural unity of the poem, as differentiated from the formal unity, lies not so much in a division of the

---

1. For example, see Buckley, *Tennyson:* "*In Memoriam* itself, as a finished 'piece of art,' is designed so that its many parts may subserve a single meaningful 'end,' a distinct if rather diffuse pattern of movement from death to life, from dark to light" (p. 119); quoted by Bishop, "The Unity of 'In Memoriam,'" p. 9.

poem into four parts divided by the three Christmases, as in an
Aristotelian tripartite division into a beginning, a middle, and
an end.

*

As I suggested in the preceding chapter, it is my belief that
Hallam operates in *In Memoriam* in much the same way that
Beatrice operates in the *Vita Nuova* and the *Divine Comedy;*
that is, he is at once a reality and the poem's central symbol. Hallam functions in the poem, in Maurice's terms, as the means
through which the persona ascends to knowledge of the divine. In
this role Hallam is fused with Christ, a fusion which is made explicit in the Prologue, written in 1849, but established in sections
composed earlier. In the Prologue the poet addresses "Strong Son
of God, immortal Love":

> Forgive my grief for one removed,
>> Thy creature, whom I found so fair.
>> I trust he lives in thee, and there
> I find him worthier to be loved.

The poet explicitly states that he trusts Hallam has been fused
with Christ and is thereby worthier of love. The same suggestion
is made in the epithalamium, written at least as early as 1845,[2]
"That friend of mine who lives in God." As early as section VII
of the poem, as we have seen,[3] this fusion is suggested by the poet,
but unperceived by the persona. An analysis of the images of
sense in *In Memoriam* will show how such a fusion is prepared
for and rendered.

Though the hand image has been discussed by others,[4] it is
necessary to discuss it and other images of sense here, because it

2. Edmund Lushington saw the manuscript in the summer of 1845. For a
conjectural dating of the epithalamium see Mattes, *"In Memoriam": The Way
of a Soul,* p. 124, and Ricks, *Poems,* p. 981n.

3. See p. 39.

4. See, for example, Bradley, *A Commentary,* pp. 42–48; Charles Richard
Sanders, "Tennyson and the Human Hand," *VN,* no. 11 (1957): 5–14; Bishop,
"The Unity of 'In Memoriam,'" p. 12; Buckley, *Tennyson,* p. 114; Mattes, *"In
Memoriam": The Way of a Soul,* p. 49 and *n;* Ryals, *Theme and Symbol,* p. 201;
and Langbaum, *The Modern Spirit,* p. 61.

is through these images that the fusion and transformation of Hallam into Christ can most clearly be seen. The images of the *hand, touch, clasping,* and *reaching,* coupled with images of the *voice* and *hearing* and the *eye* and *seeing,* appear specifically in the poem almost two hundred times. If we add to them the associated images of the *door* and *entering,* we have an impressive total through which a pattern is established.[5]

The movement of the poem is from isolation to union: in the beginning hands reach in vain, sight is lost, the voice is no longer heard, doors are approached and found closed. As the persona advances spiritually, the doors open, the voice is heard, and the hand is clasped; it is not, however, the lost hand and voice of Hallam, but the hand and voice of Christ.

In section I the persona asks,

> But who shall so forecast the years
> And find in loss a gain to match?
> Or reach a hand through time to catch
> The far-off interest of tears?

The answer to the question is all those who accept Christ as love and specifically the persona himself, who is able through the agency of Hallam to reach his hand through time and gather just such interest. In section LXXX the persona asserts that had he died first, Hallam would have turned just such loss into gain: [6]

> I make a picture in the brain;
> I hear the sentence that he speaks;
> He bears the burthen of the weeks
> But turns his burthen into gain.

5. These words are not, of course, always used for their imagistic value in the poem; that is, they are often used quite literally, e.g., "all within was noise / Of songs, and clapping hands" (LXXXVII).

6. Tennyson voices the same sentiment in *The Sisters,* published in 1880:

> . . . My God, I would not live
> Save that I think this gross hard-seeming world
> Is our misshaping vision of the Powers
> Behind the world, that make our griefs our gains.   (223–26)

Hallam Tennyson tells us in the *Memoir* that his father quoted these lines as his belief (p. 629).

> His credit thus shall set me free;
> And, influence-rich to soothe and save,
> Unused example from the grave
> Reach out dead hands to comfort me.

As we shall see, the persona finds in the loss of Hallam a gain to match in Christ. His loss is physical, but his gain is spiritual.

It is certainly not Nature which provides such a gain, for in section III Nature is described as "A hollow form with empty hands." The persona errs when he seeks the physical Hallam. When he first goes to Hallam's house (VII), the images of the hand and the door are associated:

> Doors, where my heart was used to beat
> So quickly, waiting for a hand,
>
> A hand that can be clasped no more—. . . .

Hallam, the personal form, is beyond reach; the door is closed against him.[7] The hand and the voice, the symbols of earthly union, are again and again denied him. The persona is no longer able to touch those "hands so often clasped in mine" (x); "where warm hands have prest and closed" there is now only "Silence" (XIII).[8] The reason is that "The human-hearted man [he] loved" has become "A Spirit, not a breathing voice" (XIII), has become, as the poem later establishes, fused with Christ, a spirit nobler and worthier to be loved.

The transformation of the sense images from the physical to the spiritual is prepared for from the beginning. As we have seen above, the hand very early in the poem is associated with Hallam. In section XIV the transformation of the hand is perhaps hinted at:

> And if along with these should come
> The man I held as half-divine;

---

7. In John 10:9 Christ describes himself as the door: "I am the door: by me if any man enter in, he shall be saved, and shall go in and out, and find pasture." In the poem the persona must go through Christ again to reach Hallam; paradoxically, he must also go through Hallam to reach Christ.

8. See also section XVIII, where the persona describes his life as "Treasuring the look it cannot find, / The words that are not heard again."

> Should strike a sudden hand in mine,
> And ask a thousand things of home. . . .

The hand here is of course Hallam's, but the man who is half-divine echoes the "Strong Son of God" of the Prologue, who seems "human and divine." In other words, the language used to describe Hallam and Christ is the same. Also the hand, which we have associated with Hallam, by section XXXVI we are expected to associate with Christ:

> And so the Word had breath, and wrought
> With human hands the creed of creeds
> In loveliness of perfect deeds,
> More strong than all poetic thought. . . .[9]

I do not mean to suggest that as early as section XXXVI there is any kind of union. The persona does not grasp the hand, nor is he touched by it; that comes later. It is important to note, however, that there are various hands in the early part of the poem—those of Hallam, of Christ, and of the persona—which we shall see joined later in the poem. Tennyson is preparing us for just such an eventuality. Though the persona seeks the hand of Hallam, it is really the hand of Christ which he must grasp; it is "the shining hand" of Him "that died in Holy Land" (LXXXIV). It is the persona's growth from knowledge to wisdom which makes him realize the fact, but it is a fact which the poet has realized from the beginning. The poet has, therefore, associated the hand not only with Hallam but with Christ, suggesting through the image the eventual fusing of Hallam and Christ.

Though contact is not achieved in section XXXVI, it is at least

---

9. Even earlier in the poem (section XXX) the image of touch is associated with the Father: "O Father, touch the east, and light / The light that shone when Hope was born." It is also in section XXXVI that the image of the door changes; it is no longer the door of section VII shut against the persona, but an open door which allows the entrance of truth:

> For Wisdom dealt with mortal powers,
> Where truth in closest words shall fail,
> When truth embodied in a tale
> Shall enter in at lowly doors.

suggested by section LXIX, where there seems to be a touch and a voice:

> I dreamed there would be Spring no more,
>> That Nature's ancient power was lost:
>> The streets were black with smoke and frost,
> They chattered trifles at the door:
>
> I wandered from the noisy town,
>> I found a wood with thorny boughs:
>> I took the thorns to bind my brows,
> I wore them like a civic crown:
>
> I met with scoffs, I met with scorns
>> From youth and babe and hoary hairs:
>> They called me in the public squares
> The fool that wears a crown of thorns:
>
> They called me fool, they called me child:
>> I found an angel of the night;
>> The voice was low, the look was bright;
> He looked upon my crown and smiled:
>
> He reached the glory of a hand,
>> That seemed to touch it into leaf:
>> The voice was not the voice of grief,
> The words were hard to understand.

There are apparently two associations for the crown of this section—Christ's crown of thorns and the poet's crown of laurel leaves—and both are at once implicit. For Christ the crown of thorns, symbolizing suffering, sorrow, and death, is prelude to the crown of life; so in the poem, for the persona, the crown of thorns, symbolizing death, is touched into leaf, symbolizing life. It is because of the promise of the resurrection that the angel's "look was bright" and his "voice was not the voice of grief." The dream is a revelation of immortality; the Christian overtones of the crown of thorns are too palpable to ignore. And though the persona finds the dream hard to understand, it seems to me that the reader is expected to understand. I think the crown can also be understood to refer to the laurel crown of the poet: the crown of thorns, the suffering occasioned by the death of Hallam, is touched into leaf; it comes to fruition in the poem—*In Memoriam*. Though the death of Hallam occasions the sorrow of the crown of thorns, it is also the occasion for turning that crown into the laurel crown, for turning the persona into a poet. In a sense the persona has turned the loss of Hallam into gain in poetry. The touch and the voice, then, which are sought by the persona come in section LXIX, but they come in a dream, a dream not fully understood.[10]

In section CXIX the persona makes a second trip to Hallam's house:

> Doors, where my heart was used to beat
> So quickly, not as one that weeps
> I come once more; the city sleeps;
> I smell the meadow in the street;
>
> I hear a chirp of birds; I see
> Betwixt the black fronts long-withdrawn
> A light-blue lane of early dawn,
> And think of early days and thee,
>
> And bless thee, for thy lips are bland,
> And bright the friendship of thine eye;
> And in my thoughts with scarce a sigh
> I take the pressure of thine hand.

The sense imagery has shifted. No longer is he denied contact, but the contact is spiritual, not physical. The hand that he takes he takes in his thoughts, and it is the hand at once of Hallam and Christ.[11] There is union, but it is spiritual union, not the physical reunion that the persona had sought early in the poem. The hand here is clearly Hallam's, but the fusion of Hallam and Christ makes it little different from the shining hand of section LXXXIV

10. Critics do not all attempt to analyze this dream sequence. A. C. Bradley says of the section, "It is not likely that the reader is expected to interpret the details of the dream" (*A Commentary*, p. 162). Ryals, who apparently agrees with Bradley, goes a step further: "I frankly admit that I do not understand what this passage means, nor do I think that the reader is meant to understand" (*Theme and Symbol*, p. 226). Of the passage Tennyson said, "To write poems about death and grief is 'to wear a crown of thorns,' which the people say ought to be laid aside" (Eversley Edition of the *Works*, 3:243).

11. The fusion of Hallam and Christ, as we saw, was suggested in section VII, the section dealing with the *first* trip to Hallam's house. See p. 39.

or the hands which come out of darkness, reach through nature, and mould men (cxxiv). In a sense Hallam has moulded the persona just as Christ has moulded the persona; both have made him man. Both, too, have in communion with the persona made the poem, as is suggested by the implied hand image of section cxxv:

> Whatever I have said or sung,
>   Some bitter notes my harp would give,
>   Yea, though there often seemed to live
> A contradiction on the tongue,
>
> Yet Hope had never lost her youth;
>   She did but look through dimmer eyes;
>   Or Love but played with gracious lies,
> Because he felt so fixed in truth:
>
> And if the song were full of care,
>   He breathed the spirit of the song;
>   And if the words were sweet and strong
> He set his royal signet there;
>
> Abiding with me till I sail
>   To seek thee on the mystic deeps,
>   And this electric force, that keeps
> A thousand pulses dancing, fail.

Clearly we may legitimately understand the hand of Love, which bears the royal signet, to be the hand of Christ, who we are told in the Prologue is "Strong Son of God, immortal Love." The "He" (Christ), who bears the royal signet, is differentiated from the "thee" (Hallam), who will eventually be sought by the persona on the mystic deeps. And though we are told here that the hand of Christ is on the poem, we know that the hand of Hallam is also on the poem. Hallam is the human occasion and Christ the divine occasion for *In Memoriam,* and the search for Hallam ends with Christ, who will abide with the persona until death.

A second set of images, like the images of sense already discussed, is also to be associated with Christ. They are the images of the *fool* and the *child.* In the Prologue the persona says,

> . . . . We are fools and slight;
> We mock thee when we do not fear:
> But help thy foolish ones to bear;
> Help thy vain worlds to bear thy light.

There are perhaps paradoxically two kinds of fools here: the fool of Proverbs 1:7, "The fear of the Lord is the beginning of knowledge: but fools despise wisdom and instruction," and the fool of I Cor. 3:18, "Let no man deceive himself. If any man among you seemeth to be wise in this world, let him become a fool, that he may be wise." Both texts are perhaps appropriate comments on the poem, but it is the second kind of fool particularly which we are to associate with the persona: he is the fool who seeks wisdom; he is the child who seeks his father.[12] The fool and the child are indeed related in the dream sequence of section LXIX, quoted above, the section in which the persona is described as "The fool that wears the crown of thorns: / They called me fool, they called me child." The persona is a fool in the eyes of the world, but that foolishness leads to wisdom. The persona is also a child, but as Christ says in Matt. 18:3, "Except ye be converted, and become as little children, ye shall not enter into the kingdom of heaven."

In section CIX the suggestion is again made that the way to wisdom is through becoming as a child; in that section the persona sees himself as a child in relation to Hallam, who is wise:

> And manhood fused with female grace
> In such a sort, the child would twine
> A trustful hand, unasked, in thine,
> And find his comfort in thy face;
>
> All these have been, and thee mine eyes
> Have looked on: if they looked in vain,
> My shame is greater who remain,
> Nor let thy wisdom make me wise.

12. Tennyson seems to have had this passage in mind in a remark to Rawnsley in 1884. Someone had written "Old Tennyson is a fool" on his gate; Tennyson said, "The boy's about right; we are all of us fools, if we only knew it. We are but at the beginning of wisdom" (H. D. Rawnsley, *Memories of the Tennysons* [Glasgow, 1900], p. 100) .

The persona's knowledge of the physical Hallam should be his means to wisdom, his means to the spiritual. But Hallam is at the same time a physical reflection of the spiritual, as the poet gives him the attributes of Christ in "manhood fused with female grace." In the *Memoir* we are told that Tennyson saw in Christ's infinite pity "what he called 'the man-woman' in Christ, the union of tenderness and strength." [13] Through the knowledge of Hallam the persona can be made wise; through the natural, which reflects the spiritual, he can progress toward the spiritual— that is, he can progress from knowledge to wisdom through becoming as a child. In section CXXIV, where the persona speaks of the time "when faith had fallen asleep," he suggests again the movement to wisdom through becoming as a child:

> No, like a child in doubt and fear:
>   But that blind clamour made me wise;
>   Then was I as a child that cries,
> But, crying, knows his father near.

In section CXIV the poet makes explicit the relationship between knowledge and wisdom, and he does so through the use of the images of the hand and the child:

> Who loves not Knowledge? Who shall rail
>   Against her beauty? May she mix
>   With men and prosper! Who shall fix
> Her pillars? Let her work prevail.
>
> But on her forehead sits a fire:
>   She sets her forward countenance
>   And leaps into the future chance,
> Submitting all things to desire.
>
> Half-grown as yet, a child, and vain—
>   She cannot fight the fear of death.
>   What is she, cut from love and faith,
> But some wild Pallas from the brain

13. P. 274*n.* Killham in *Tennyson and "The Princess,"* p. 260, Smith, *The Two Voices,* p. 155, and Ricks, *Poems,* p. 962*n,* associate this passage in *In Memoriam* with the attributes of Christ given in the *Memoir.*

Of Demons? fiery-hot to burst
  All barriers in her onward race
  For power. Let her know her place;
She is the second, not the first.

A higher hand must make her mild,
  If all be not in vain; and guide
  Her footsteps, moving side by side
With wisdom, like the younger child:

For she is earthly of the mind,
  But Wisdom heavenly of the soul.
  O, friend, who camest to thy goal
So early, leaving me behind,

I would the great world grew like thee,
  Who grewest not alone in power
  And knowledge, but by year and hour
In reverence and in charity.[14]

The higher hand, which has been identified in the poem with Christ, is the means by which knowledge is made mild, the means by which knowledge is taught to walk with wisdom. The distinction made here is not very different from Carlyle's "Thought without Reverence is barren" or Julius Hare's "Knowledge is the parent of love; Wisdom, love itself." [15] Tennyson himself had made similar distinctions in other early poems, for example in *Love thou thy land* (1833):

>   Make knowledge circle with the winds;
>   But let her herald, Reverence, fly
>   Before her to whatever sky
>   Bear seed of men and growth of minds.   (17–20)

and in *Love and Duty* (1842):

----

14. The opening quatrain of this section is repeated verbatim from "Hail Briton!" (1831–33). See Donahue, "Tennyson's 'Hail, Briton!' and 'Tithon,'" p. 390, and Ricks, *Poems,* p. 966n.

15. *Sartor Resartus,* ed. C. F. Harrold (New York, 1937), p. 68; *Guesses at Truth: First Series,* p. 80.

> . . . . Wait, and Love himself will bring
> The drooping flower of knowledge changed to fruit
> Of wisdom. . . .   (23–25)

At any rate, an examination of the human images has perhaps established the function of Hallam in the poem and the
relation between him and the persona. In addition it has suggested in part at least the relationship between knowledge and
wisdom. The second relationship is developed more fully through
other natural images.

*

One group of natural images appear in the poem in pairs,
and the members of the pairs are antithetical. For example, a
dominant pair of images is light and dark. To these should be
added related pairs of images, such as the fire and the cloud, the
morning and evening stars, calm and storm. If the movement of
the poem were, as has often been suggested, a movement from
despair to faith, one could reasonably expect the poem to begin
in darkness and move toward light. And yet that is not the case.
Darkness is not transformed into light, but rather remains darkness, which is harmonized with light. The random mingling of
images with which the poem begins moves toward balance rather
than toward the elimination of one of the pairs of images. Though
the persona comes to perceive that there is a "Unity of Nature
. . . behind the cosmic process of matter in motion and changing forms of life," the cosmic process itself does not cease. Darkness is not denied by the persona, but is accepted as a manifestation of the same power which manifests itself in light.

An examination of three early sections will perhaps make
clearer the confusion and conflict which are eventually perceived
as order. Section xi deals with the calm of nature, a calm which
is associated with morning and light:

> Calm is the morn without a sound,
>   Calm as to suit a calmer grief,
>   And only through the faded leaf
> The chestnut pattering to the ground:

Calm and deep peace on this high wold,
  And on these dews that drench the furze,
  And all the silvery gossamers
That twinkle into green and gold:

Calm and still light on yon great plain
  That sweeps with all its autumn bowers,
  And crowded farms and lessening towers,
To mingle with the bounding main:

Calm and deep peace in this wide air,
  These leaves that redden to the fall;
  And in my heart, if calm at all,
If any calm, a calm despair:

Calm on the seas, and silver sleep,
  And waves that sway themselves in rest,
  And dead calm in that noble breast
Which heaves but with the heaving deep.

Section xv is clearly a companion section and deals with the
storm in nature, and the storm is associated with night:

Tonight the winds begin to rise
  And roar from yonder dropping day:
  The last red leaf is whirled away,
The rooks are blown about the skies;

The forest cracked, the waters curled,
  The cattle huddled on the lea;
  And wildly dashed on tower and tree
The sunbeam strikes along the world:

And but for fancies, which aver
  That all thy motions gently pass
  Athwart a plane of molten glass,
I scarce could brook the strain and stir

That makes the barren branches loud;
  And but for fear it is not so,
  The wild unrest that lives in woe
Would dote and pore on yonder cloud

That rises upward always higher,
 And onward drags a labouring breast,
 And topples round the dreary west,
A looming bastion fringed with fire.

We have in these two sections, then, light, calm, morn, on the one hand, and dark, storm, and night on the other.[16] Another pair of images is also introduced—the images of the cloud and the fire. These last images are related in the poem to day and night as they echo the relation in Exodus 13:21: "And the Lord went before them by day in a pillar of a cloud, to lead them the way; and by night in a pillar of fire, to give them light; to go by day and night." What the persona eventually comes to realize is that God is in the cloud and the fire,[17] the light and the dark, is in storm and night as well as in calm and day. It is this which the Prologue asserts of Christ: "Thine are these orbs of light and shade; / Thou madest Life in man and brute; / Thou madest Death"; and it is this which the development of the images in the poem reinforces. As the persona must learn to accept death, he must learn to accept darkness, storm, and so on. If God made life, he

16. Tennyson had addressed himself to the antitheses of the phenomenal world even before the death of Hallam; see his use of the same images in *Song* ("Every day hath its night," 1830) :

Golden calm and storm
 Mingle day by day.
There is no bright form
Doth not cast a shade—

17. In *The Two Voices,* in lines apparently written in 1835–37 (see Ricks, *Poems,* p. 522) , Tennyson uses the same metaphor to describe the spiritual behind the natural:

So heavenly-toned, that in that hour
From out my sullen heart a power
Broke, like the rainbow from the shower,

To feel, although no tongue can prove,
That every cloud, that spreads above
And veileth love, itself is love. (442–47)

The speaker in *Despair* (1881) uses the same image to deny God:

We had past from a cheerless night to the glare of a drearier day;
He is only a cloud and a smoke who was once a pillar of fire,
The guess of a worm in the dust and the shadow of its desire—
                                                                      (28–30)

also made death, and all the apparent contrarieties of the phenomenal world can be reconciled in the acceptance of them as diverse manifestations of God's unity.

That we are to associate light and dark with life and death as manifestations of God's unity is apparent in the lines quoted above from the Prologue. But as early as section XVI the persona does not see clearly that all is one in Christ; he therefore questions how "Can calm despair and wild unrest / Be tenants of a single breast, / Or sorrow such a changeling be?" Shock has made him "that delirious man / Whose fancy fuses old and new, / And flashes into false and true, / And mingles all without a plan." All is confusion and chaos; there is no balance, no harmony. The world appears to be a random mingling of opposing forces without plan. But even here, this early, the seeds of perception are present in the persona: he "scarce could brook the strain and stir" if it were not for "fancies, which aver / That all [Nature's] motions gently pass / Athwart a plane of molten glass" (xv). These last lines appear to echo I Cor. 13:12, "For now we see through a glass, darkly; but then face to face: now I know in part; but then shall I know even as also I am known." If the persona does not see clearly, perhaps the poet is preparing us for his eventual recognition that to know in part leads one to accept a coherent whole, for the persona comes to conclude, "I see in part / That all, as in some piece of art, / Is toil cöoperant to an end" (CXXVIII).

The images of this cluster, then, appear together early in the poem, but not in harmony. For example, in section IX, one of the earliest written sections,[18] night is succeeded by "Phosphor, bright," and in the following section the persona hears "the bell struck in the night," but also sees "the cabin-window bright." Light and dark appear together but distinct, and there is no perception of their essential unity by the persona. In the same way, as we have seen, the cloud and the fire of section xv appear together, but not in harmony. In section xxx, one of the first Christmas sections, the images of night and morn, the cloud and the "seraphic flame" are mingled, but not related to one another. And so it is again and again early in the poem.

18. This section is dated October 6, 1833. See Mattes, *"In Memoriam": The Way of a Soul*, p. 113, and Ricks, *Poems*, p. 872*n*.

The second yew tree section (XXXIX, added to the poem in 1869) suggests a blending of the images. The yew is the dark yew of section II, but now it gives off a "fruitful cloud" of pollen to the random stroke of the persona's walking stick; even the yew has its "golden hour" when its "gloom is kindled at the tips." Here the cloud and the fire are implicitly blended rather than random or conflicting. So perhaps are the images of dark and light as the gloom is kindled in the golden hour. Moreover, the suggestion of the blending of life and death is apparent in that we have the traditionally funereal yew tree coming to fruition, denying the persona's assertion in the first yew tree section that the tree will neither glow nor bloom nor change. The persona of course seems unaware of the significance of the blending of the images. As the persona's perception increases with the progress of the poem, however, the harmonization of the images becomes more explicit.

Section XCV has long been seen as a crucial section. As the dead man touches him from the past, the persona has a vision, similar in some ways to the vision of Adam in Book XI (ll. 370 ff.) of *Paradise Lost.* The persona says,

> And all at once it seemed at last
> The living soul was flashed on mine,
>
> And mine in this was wound, and whirled
> About empyreal heights of thought,
> And came on that which is, and caught
> The deep pulsations of the world,
>
> Æonian music measuring out
> The steps of Time—the shocks of Chance—
> The blows of Death. . . .

The "living soul" is traditionally the first Adam,[19] who precedes the "quickening spirit," the second Adam, Christ (I Cor. 15:45). In a way, Hallam in the poem is like Adam, in that he is the natural man who precedes and promises the spiritual man. Adam,

---

19. Tennyson himself was apparently somewhat confused about the meaning behind "the living soul." He said, "The Deity, maybe. The first reading, 'his living soul,' troubled me, as perhaps giving a wrong impression" (Eversley Edition of *Works,* 3:251–52).

when he is taken by Michael to the mountain to envision subsequent history, sees also "The steps of Time—the shocks of Chance — / The blows of Death." Such a vision is followed for Adam by the vision of Christ. In a like manner perhaps, a similar kind of vision in this section of *In Memoriam* ends, if not specifically with Christ, at least in hope with a merging of contradictory images in unity, a unity which I suggest is spiritual:

> And East and West, without a breath,
> Mixt their dim lights, like life and death,
> To broaden into boundless day.

What the persona comes to realize is that East and West, light and dark, life and death are all manifestations of the oneness of God. He learns that God made both life and death, as the Prologue states and the following section (xcvi) reaffirms:

> And Power was with him in the night,
> Which makes the darkness and the light,
> And dwells not in the light alone,
>
> But in the darkness and the cloud,
> As over Sinaï's peaks of old,
> While Israel made their gods of gold,
> Although the trumpet blew so loud.[20]

From here on in the poem the images which the persona's knowledge told him were diverse are regularly seen as unified because his wisdom allows him to see them as such. In section ciii, for example, the cloud becomes a "crimson cloud," merging the cloud and the fire. In section cxii the persona's love for Hallam has brought him the wisdom to see

> Large elements in order brought,
> And tracts of calm from tempest made,
> And world-wide fluctuation swayed
> In vassal tides that followed thought.

20. This section also echoes parts of Books XI and XII of *Paradise Lost,* indicating perhaps that Tennyson had those books in mind when he wrote sections xcv and xcvi.

The persona does not deny change but accepts it because he sees order in it. The "cosmic process of matter in motion" continues, but it is seen as truly cosmic rather than chaotic.

The unity of apparent diversity is made most clear in CXXI:

> Sad Hesper o'er the buried sun
>   And ready, thou, to die with him,
>   Thou watchest all things ever dim
> And dimmer, and a glory done:
>
> The team is loosened from the wain,
>   The boat is drawn upon the shore;
>   Thou listenest to the closing door,
> And life is darkened in the brain.
>
> Bright Phosphor, fresher for the night,
>   By thee the world's great work is heard
>   Beginning, and the wakeful bird;
> Behind thee comes the greater light:
>
> The market boat is on the stream,
>   And voices hail it from the brink;
>   Thou hear'st the village hammer clink,
> And see'st the moving of the team.
>
> Sweet Hesper-Phosphor, double name
>   For what is one, the first, the last,
>   Thou, like my present and my past,
> Thy place is changed; thou art the same.

Of the five quatrains of this section the first two are devoted to Hesper, the evening star—to sadness, darkness, night, passivity, ending, and death. The second two are devoted to Phosphor, the morning star—to freshness, light, day, activity, beginning, life. The fifth quatrain merges the previous four. Hesper and Phosphor are seen to be two names for the same star, which indeed they are. Though they, and their related activities or lack of activities, appear to be different, they are really one; their place alone is changed (or seems to be changed). They are unity manifesting itself in diversity.

There are, however, other names for this same star which make the associative images even more complex. Hesper is also called

Venus, who, of course, is the pagan goddess of love. Phosphor, on the other hand, is also Christ, who describes himself as the morning star in Rev. 22:16: "I Jesus have sent mine angel to testify unto you these things in the churches. I am the root and the offspring of David, and the bright and morning star." In Venus, the pagan goddess of love, and Christ, the Christian God of love, we have perhaps diverse manifestations of the same thing, both the natural and the spiritual manifestations. It is certainly likely that Tennyson expects us to associate "Sweet Hesper-Phosphor" with Christ, as he describes the star as "the first, the last," and Christ says of himself also in Rev. 22:13, "I am Alpha and Omega, the beginning and the end, the first and the last." Christ is also "the greater light" which follows Phosphor, as he is traditionally symbolized by the sun. He is at once Phosphor, Hesper, and the sun; all, like the persona's present and his past, merge here in one. They find their unity in Christ, for, as the persona says, "Sweet Hesper-Phosphor [is a] double name / For what is one, the first, the last." And the one who is *one,* who is first and last, is Christ.[21]

The merging seen in section cxxi is reiterated in section cxxx where the persona says of the Hallam-Christ figure, "Thou standest in the rising sun, / And in the setting thou art fair." Hallam is found in both the rising and the setting sun, and associated with the related images of light and dark and life and death, because these are all manifestations of God, and Hallam is, as this section tells us, "mixed with God and Nature." Moreover, the comment on the *fairness* of Hallam–Christ may mean that he is both beautiful and just.[22] Such a reading of these lines accords with the third quatrain of the Prologue, where the justice of Christ, who "madest Death," is affirmed:

> Thou wilt not leave us in the dust:
>   Thou madest man, he knows not why,
>   He thinks he was not made to die;
> And thou hast made him: thou art just.

21. Bradley suggests that "what is one" refers to "Love." He goes on to say, "The next words may be intended to recall, 'I am Alpha and Omega, the first and the last,' Rev. i, 11" (*Commentary,* p. 218). See also Ricks, *Poems,* p. 972n.

22. I am indebted to Herman M. Levy for pointing out this pun to me. Ricks (*Poems,* p. 979n) compares this passage to Rev. 19:17: "And I saw an angel standing in the sun."

By the end of the poem, at least, the persona can accept diversity because he trusts that it is a manifestation of unity; he can accept change because he trusts that behind it there is permanence.[23]

Still other paired images, which do not appear as antithetical, reflect the persona's developing attitude toward change rather than diversity: they are *dust* and *ashes*. *Dust* appears many times in the poem, from the Prologue to the final section before the epithalamium, and it has obvious associations with death. In the Prologue, as we have seen, the persona says that Christ will "not leave us in the dust"; later (xxi) Hallam's body is described as "sacred dust." *Dust* is also associated with death in sections xvii, xxxiv, xxxv, lxxx, and cv; but in section lxxi the persona speaks of "the dust of change," suggesting prehaps that dust or death is to be seen as change rather than ending. And so it would seem in the spring song of section cxvi:

> Is it, then, regret for buried time
> > That keenlier in sweet April wakes,
> > And meets the year, and gives and takes
> The colours of the crescent prime?
>
> Not all: the songs, the stirring air,
> > The life re-orient out of dust,
> > Cry through the sense to hearten trust
> In that which made the world so fair.

Here dust, which has been associated with death, is associated with life. Indeed the sense which sees "life re-orient out of dust" in nature leads the persona to trust in the spirit "which made the world so fair." Such a suggestion of possible life from ashes in nature, if not from dust, was sensed as early as section xviii, without,

23. His acceptance of change is suggested as early as section xxx:

> Once more we sang: 'They do not die
> Nor lose their mortal sympathy,
> Nor change to us, although they change. . . .'

See also section xlvii:

> Eternal form shall still divide
> The eternal soul from all beside;
> And I shall know him when we meet:

and section lxi, where first form and second form are distinguished.

however, the consequent trust in the spirit: "And from his ashes may be made / The violet of his native land." Those ashes which *may* produce the violet in section XVIII *do* produce the violet in the spring song of section CXV:

> Now fades the last long streak of snow,
>   Now burgeons every maze of quick
>   About the flowering squares, and thick
> By ashen roots the violets blow.

The imagery of death as stasis of section XVI, a section in which change is questioned, is also transformed in section CXV. In section XVI (partially quoted above) the persona asks,

> What words are these have fallen from me?
>   Can calm despair and wild unrest
>   Be tenants of a single breast,
> Or sorrow such a changeling be?
>
> Or doth she only seem to take
>   The touch of change in calm or storm;
>   But knows no more of transient form
> In her deep self, than some dead lake
>
> That holds the shadow of a lark
>   Hung in the shadow of a heaven?

In section CXV his question is answered:

> Now rings the woodland loud and long,
>   The distance takes a lovelier hue,
>   And drowned in yonder living blue
> The lark becomes a sightless song.

The sense of touch, which we have come to associate in the poem with Christ, may perhaps be associated here in the same way. Christ's touch is the touch of change; it is his touch which makes life re-orient out of dust, which produces from ashes the violet; it is his touch which can transform the shadow of a heaven into a living blue and the shadow of a lark into a sightless song. It is the persona's acquisition of wisdom that leads him to accept "transient form" as divinely ordained. He can accept it because he trusts that only the form changes and must change but the spiritual unity behind that form remains constant. It is only by accepting change that the persona can accept death; it is only by accepting change that he can see Hallam as "a noble type" and the "herald of a higher race"; it is only by accepting change that we can "Ring in the Christ that is to be"; it is only through change that "the whole creation" can move toward "one far-off divine event," that it can fulfill God's providential plan. The dust of death, the persona hopes, will give way to eternal life, the dust of change to permanence.

*

Finally, and briefly, *In Memoriam* has in addition to its formal unity a structural unity which is more than and different from "the unity and continuity of a diary," precisely because it is aesthetically controlled. Borrowing Aristotle's definition of a tragedy, one could say that *In Memoriam* "is an imitation of an action that is complete, and whole, and of a certain magnitude." The action which it imitates is the action of one under the blight of a great sorrow who progresses spiritually from knowledge to wisdom, but it is an imitation rather than a record. Its wholeness resides in part in the fact that it imitates a single action, though the persona's progress is not straight forward and without reversals. Its wholeness also resides in the fact that structurally it conforms to Aristotle's definition of the whole: "A whole is that which has a beginning, a middle, and an end. A beginning is that which does not itself follow anything by causal necessity, but after which something naturally is or comes to be. An end, on the contrary, is that which itself naturally follows some other thing, either by necessity, or as a rule, but has nothing following it. A middle is that which follows something as some other thing follows it." [24]

I have rather dragged Aristotle in by the heels because the

---

24. *Poetics,* trans. S. H. Butcher, in *The Great Critics* (New York, 1951), p. 36. Arnold "described *In Memoriam* as the archetype of 'poems which have no beginning, middle or end, but are holdings forth in verse, which, for anything in the nature of the composition itself, may perfectly well go on for ever'" (quoted in Sidney M. B. Coulling, "Matthew Arnold's 1853 Preface: Its Origin and Aftermath," *VS,* 7 [1964]: 238).

unity of *In Memoriam* has so often been denied or so vaguely discussed that some clarification seems necessary. Moreover, the relations between the parts of the poem have been disputed or confused. Mrs. Mattes, for example, seems to feel that the Prologue has little to do with the poem, that it "reflects a different religious attitude from that of the poems which it introduces," and she suggests that there is a "new, evangelical note" introduced perhaps to impress Emily Sellwood and Henry Hallam.[25] And E. K. Brown reflects at least one school of thought in his contention that "This Prologue is properly the conclusion of *In Memoriam*." [26]

On the contrary, the Prologue is neither irrelevant nor misleading, nor is it properly the conclusion. It is the beginning of the poem. The Prologue is the key to the poem, the guide to the labyrinth. It is the Prologue that suggests the direction the poem will take and the meaning it will have. The obvious Christianity of the Prologue is not a new note, nor does it reflect "a different religious attitude from the poems which it introduces"; it rather clarifies the palpable Christianity of later sections of the poem as we have seen. The Prologue merely states more explicitly what the poem as a whole develops metaphorically.[27] The fact that the Prologue was written last is neither improper nor I should think unusual in a work of art. It is the critical insistence that *In Memoriam* is some kind of a diary and not a work of art which has led to the confusion.

Like the Prologue, the epithalamium, with which the poem concludes and about which little has so far been said, is an essential part of the poem. It is the poem's almost inevitable conclusion, not because it is within the tradition of the pastoral elegy, not because it is the autobiographical ending to an autobiographical

25. *In Memoriam: The Way of a Soul*, pp. 90, 91. I would argue that the Prologue does not introduce "poems" at all, but a single poem, of which it is a part.

26. *Victorian Poetry*, ed. E. K. Brown and J. O. Bailey, 2d ed. (New York, 1962), p. 742. See also Smith, *The Two Voices*: "The Prologue, written last, is a summary and digest of the thought of the whole, rather than an introduction to it" (pp. 88–89); Ryals, *Theme and Symbol*: "the Prologue is the last stage in Tennyson's 'way of the soul'" (p. 268); and Pitt, *Tennyson Laureate*: "The Prologue is an after-thought . . ." (p. 115).

27. Cf. August, "Tennyson and Teilhard": "Tennyson's Prologue . . . is no more an inconsistency or an afterthought than Teilhard's Epilogue [in *The Phenomenon of Man*]" (p. 223).

poem, and not because "the theory that evolution might fulfil the dream of 'a grand crowning race' gave particular importance to marriage and the family." [28] The epithalamium is the proper conclusion for a poem which has all along moved toward fusion, toward oneness, which a wedding symbolizes. The wedding which the epithalamium celebrates is more than a wedding, however: it is a symbol of unity and it is the persona's final reconciliation to death and to change.

To see death as a wedding is, of course, a tradition in Christian literature; to see a wedding as a funeral is certainly less common, but in Tennyson's mind the two were apparently equatable. In *To H.R.H. Princess Beatrice* Tennyson wrote in 1855, "The Mother weeps / At that white funeral of the single life, / Her maiden daughter's marriage." [29] Weddings and funerals at any rate obviously came together in his mind. That we are to see death as a wedding in *In Memoriam* is made clear early in the poem. In section XL, a section which Mrs. Mattes suggests should be dated 1836,[30] the persona expresses his desire to see death in just such terms:

> Could we forget the widowed hour
>   And look on Spirits breathed away,
>   As on a maiden in the day
> When first she wears her orange-flower!
>
> When crowned with blessing she doth rise
>   To take her latest leave of home,
>   And hopes and light regrets that come
> Make April of her tender eyes;
>
> And doubtful joys the father move,
>   And tears are on the mother's face,

---

28. Killham, *Tennyson and "The Princess,"* p. 263.
29. Cf. *The Ancient Sage:*

> I hate the black negation of the bier,
> And wish the dead, as happier than ourselves
> And higher, having climbed one step beyond
> Our village miseries, might be borne in white
> To burial or to burning, hymned from hence
> With songs in praise of death, and crowned with flowers!

                                                              (204–9)

30. *"In Memoriam": The Way of a Soul,* p. 118.

> As parting with a long embrace
> She enters other realms of love;
>
> Her office there to rear, to teach,
>> Becoming as is meet and fit
>> A link among the days, to knit
> The generations each with each;
>
> And, doubtless, unto thee is given
>> A life that bears immortal fruit
>> In those great offices that suit
> The full-grown energies of heaven.

The persona's wish in section XL is to look upon those who have died as one looks upon maidens entering into "other realms of love." The epithalamium is the fulfillment of the persona's wish. By the end of the poem he can "look on Spirits breathed away" as if they were maidens approaching the consummation of a wedding. Indeed, the epithalamium is a triple consummation: it is literally a celebration of the consummation of the love of Tennyson's sister and Edmund Lushington. It is, second, the symbolic celebration of death as consummation which allows the entrance into "other realms of love," a consummation which "bears immortal fruit." To fail to see the wedding as symbolic of death is to ignore section XL; it is to ignore the relevance of the conclusion to the elegaic nature of the poem. And finally the epithalamium is the consummation of the poem. Not only is it a reflection of the unity which the persona has sought throughout the poem; it is the final resolution of the poem. It is the event toward which the whole poem moves.

In a very real sense, then, the Prologue leads to the body of the poem as the epithalamium succeeds from it. The Aristotelian demands of a beginning, a middle, and an end are satisfied and the poem is structurally sound. The structure of *In Memoriam,* no less than its form, contributes to its unity.

4. *Maud*

*T*H E history of the composition of *Maud* is a greatly confused one. At the suggestion of either H. D. Rawnsley's
mother or Sir John Simeon, or someone else, or no one at all,
Tennyson surrounded an early lyric with other lyrics, forming
thereby what he called a monodrama.[1] The original lyric, "O
that 'twere possible," published in *The Tribute* in 1837, was
apparently written in 1833; *Maud; A Monodrama* was published
in 1855 and enlarged in 1856. This history, though interesting,
need not concern us here. More to my purpose are three early
lesser poems—*The Gardener's Daughter* (written in 1833 and
published in 1842), *Edwin Morris* (written in 1839 and published in 1851), and *Locksley Hall* (written 1837–38, published
1842) —because all have elements in common with *Maud*. A brief
examination of these inferior poems may prove helpful in show-
ing how material indifferently handled could be transformed by
the poet into the powerful and successful later poem.

*

The Gardener's Daughter is an English Idyl, a dramatic poem
about the love of a boy for a girl named Rose who lives in a
garden which the speaker associates with Eden. The garden has
lilies, roses, and a cedar tree, and the girl, like Cordelia in *Lear*,
seems to represent a kind of harmony:

1. Rawnsley says his mother suggested that Tennyson enlarge the fragment
from *The Tribute* (*Memories of the Tennysons*, p. 122) while Aubrey de Vere
thought it was Simeon (see *Memoir*, p. 318). Sir Charles Tennyson suggests that
Simeon wished Tennyson to republish the original fragment and that it was
Tennyson's own idea to enlarge it (see *Tennyson*, p. 281). For the whole confused
history see Rader, *Tennyson's* Maud, pp. 2–11.

> She looked: but all
> Suffused with blushes—neither self-possessed
> Nor startled, but betwixt this mood and that,
> Divided in a graceful quiet. . . .   (150–53)

The Rose among roses in the Edenic garden of *The Gardener's Daughter* is like the situation in *Maud,* and the poet introduces the same images. But in the earlier poem the images are undeveloped, the situation insufficiently dramatic. The result is a poem without life, without depth, with the power to satisfy only the most saccharine tastes.

Edwin Morris, another English Idyl, is perhaps a step forward, but it is not a very large step, and the introduction of the "fat-faced curate Edward Bull" does little to improve an already weak poem. In *Edwin Morris* a boy falls in love with a girl, Letty Hill, who if not a Rose in the Garden of Eden is "Like Proserpine in Enna" (112).[2] Love, however, does not run smoothly as in *The Gardener's Daughter;* the materialistic family of Letty Hill rejects the boy as unsuitable:

> . . . . and out they came
> Trustees and Aunts and Uncles. 'What, with him!
> Go' (shrilled the cotton-spinning chorus) ; 'him!'
> I choked. Again they shrieked the burthen—'Him!'
> Again with hands of wild rejection 'Go!—
> Girl, get you in!' She went—and in one month
> They wedded her to sixty thousand pounds,
> To lands in Kent and messuages in York,
> And slight Sir Robert with his watery smile
> And educated whisker. . . .   (120–29)

Here, then, we have in the crass materialism of family obtruding on natural, perhaps Edenic love, with disastrous results for the lovers, a situation similar to those in both *Locksley Hall* and *Maud.* Moreover, there is introduced into *Edwin Morris* a kind of baronial hall, and the hero, like the one in *Maud,* is forced to flee into exile to avoid prosecution (not to Brittany to be sure,

---

2. Tennyson, like Milton, associated the Vale of Enna with the Garden of Eden. See G. Robert Stange, "Tennyson's Mythology: A Study of *Demeter and Persephone,*" in Killham, *Critical Essays on the Poetry of Tennyson,* p. 145.

only to London). But a poem of only 147 lines in which "the fat-faced curate" is allowed to say three times "God made the woman for the man, / And for the good and increase of the world" is open to a charge of repetition, as well as irrelevance, and a lack of balance. Indeed the whole poem is confused and lacks direction; in *Edwin Morris,* as in *The Gardener's Daughter,* dramatic possibilities remain unrealized, images remain undeveloped, and the poetry is of interest only as prelude.

The amount of attention given by critics to the next anticipatory poem, *Locksley Hall,* has always surprised me, as it seems to me to be an unsuccessful poem, though it has some strengths where *The Gardener's Daughter* and *Edwin Morris* have only sentimentality. *Locksley Hall* also suffers from its sentimentality, but it is sentimental in a less cloying way. At any rate, my interest in *Locksley Hall* is primarily as a foil for *Maud:* to examine how material ineffectually handled in *Locksley Hall* but powerfully realized in *Maud* may tell us something about the later poem.

To begin with, both *Locksley Hall* and *Maud* are dramatic poems. In both, the setting includes the Hall; in *Maud* the garden is reintroduced from the earlier poems and in *Locksley Hall* it is not (though the speaker of the second poem dreams of an Oriental Eden). In both poems the speaker, son of an evil-starred father, is left an orphan. In both poems the speaker's love, in the one for his cousin Amy and in the other for Maud, is thwarted by the interference of a materialistic family. The hysteria of the speaker of *Locksley Hall* becomes perhaps the madness of the speaker of *Maud.* Here, however, the similarities end and *Maud* succeeds where *Locksley Hall* fails.

In the first place, the adolescent hero of *Locksley Hall* is a weakly realized dramatic figure. The consequence is that the reader of the poem lacks interest in what he thinks, what he does, or what he is, an interest found in the dramatic creations of Browning, for example, or in other dramatic creations of Tennyson himself. Moreover, the poet's handling of the hero is inconsistent and the poem as a whole incoherent. Are we, for instance, to take the hero's blatant egotism at the beginning of the poem as revelatory of his character and still believe him when he identifies himself a few minutes later with "Men, my brothers, men the workers" (117)? Can we be expected to take seriously the hero who fails to see the irony in "No—she never loved me truly: love is love for evermore" (74) when his own love has turned to hatred? There is no time allowed in the soliloquy for change in the character of the speaker as there is in the monodrama. It is as if Browning's monk in *The Soliloquy of the Spanish Cloister* were to end the poem with a disquisition on charity which the reader was expected to take at face value. If in *Locksley Hall* the hero's opening remarks are the result of a kind of hysteria (and such seems the most charitable interpretation), where and why does the hysteria cease and the profundity begin? If, on the other hand, the latter part of the poem is not to be taken at face value as profound, or at least straightforward, but is ironic, then generations of readers have misread it as an expression of Tennyson's hope for the future and the irony must be deemed unsuccessful.

There also seems to be too much rime for the reason and too little reason for the rime. If the shifts in subject matter in the poem are the result of hysterical adolescence on the part of the speaker, should they not still be subject to the control of the poet and subserve some dramatic purpose? And don't we have to admit that at times anyway the sound determines the sense? For example:

> Drug thy memories, lest thou learn it, lest thy heart be
>   put to proof,
> In the dead unhappy night, and when the rain is on
>   the roof.
>
> Like a dog, he hunts in dreams, and thou art staring at
>   the wall,
> Where the dying night-lamp flickers, and the shadows
>   rise and fall. (77–80)

The rather gratuitous introduction of rain on the roof and falling shadows for their rime value seems the work of a poet who nods.

My reasons for dealing with *Locksley Hall* are not, of course, to denigrate Tennyson as a poet. He has been unfortunate, I think, in that the popularity of the poem, owing perhaps to the quotability of some of the lines, has led readers to admire him for the wrong reasons—as a spokesman for his age, as a prophet, as an autobiographer—and the very real weaknesses in *Locksley*

Hall have failed to keep it from usurping the space in anthologies which could more properly be devoted to better poems. On the other hand, the poem is in some ways typical, if ineptly so. The rejection of withdrawal and the determination of a life of action with which the poem implausibly concludes is a theme dealt with successfully in many of Tennyson's early poems, but more importantly for present purposes, it is a theme subtly and richly realized in *Maud*.

My approach to *Maud* is neither psychological nor biographical and only very slightly historical.[3] My approach, though I hesitate to say it, knowing the dangers of symbol-hunting, is symbolic or perhaps imagistic. I am concerned ultimately with what the poem means and how we can know that meaning through the relations of the images and the symbolic role of Maud herself.

*

Maud, Hallam Tennyson tells us, was described by his father as " 'a little *Hamlet*,' the history of a morbid poetic soul, under the blighting influence of a recklessly speculative age. He is the heir of madness, an egotist with the makings of a cynic, raised to sanity by a pure and holy love which elevates his whole nature, passing from the height of triumph to the lowest depth of misery, driven into madness by the loss of her whom he has loved, and, when he has at length passed through the fiery furnace, and has recovered his reason, giving himself up to work for the good of mankind through the unselfishness born of his great passion." [4]

3. For the psychological approach see Roy P. Basler, "Tennyson's *Maud*," in *Sex, Symbolism and Psychology in Literature* (New Brunswick, N.J., 1948), pp. 73–93. For the biographical and psychological approach see Rader, *Tennyson's Maud*.

4. *Memoir*, p. 334. W. K. Wimsatt objects to Tennyson's description: "I myself should be quite unwilling, for instance, to make Tennyson the final interpreter ·of his own poem. The account which appears in the *Memoir* and the annotations seems to me off center in at least three respects, the emphasis on 'the holy power of Love,' that on the 'blighting influence' of a commercial age, and the idea that the poem demonstrates any final redemption through 'unselfishness.' The main force in the poem is the protagonist's riot of unhealthy emotion. The jingo theme which is planted in several early parts of the poem and provides the resolution is quite gratuitous. Tennyson's partial misreading of his own poem corresponds to the imbalance which appears in the emotions of the poem itself. His original title

Another comment, also given us by Hallam Tennyson, associates *Maud* with *In Memoriam:* "It is a 'Drama of the Soul,' set in a landscape glorified by Love, and according to Lowell, 'The antiphonal voice to "In Memoriam." ' " [5] Lowell's comment strikes me as both relevant and accurate as I think both *In Memoriam* and *Maud* are essentially religious poems about the role of love in spiritual regeneration.

In this regard, Maud is the Beatrice of the piece and plays, therefore, a role similar to that played by Hallam in *In Memoriam*. As the persona's love for the personal Hallam led him to a love for Christ, to wisdom and spiritual regeneration, so does the hero's love for Maud serve in a like way. Postponing consideration of Maud as a Beatrice figure, I should perhaps begin as the poem does with the hero and his situation.

Certainly the opening of *Maud* owes much to Carlyle's *Past and Present* (1843). In the first chapter, "Midas," Carlyle speaks of the Workhouses, which may have suggested to Tennyson those in which "the poor are hovelled and hustled together, each sex, like swine" (I, 34). More specifically, Tennyson's "Mammonite mother [who] kills her babe for a burial fee" (I, 45) appears in Carlyle's report of the Stockport Assizes, where "a Mother and Father are arraigned and found guilty of poisoning three of their children, to defraud a 'burial society' of some 3 £. 8 s. due on the death of each child." [6] The "Midas" chapter may also have suggested to Tennyson the bitter irony behind the hero's reference to "the golden age" (I, 30).

What is more important, however, than the probable source for bits and pieces of the opening of *Maud* is that Carlyle associates the materialistic corruption of England with Hell. The description of the mother and father who kill their children, for example, is preceded and followed by references to Hell. Later, in the "Gos-

---

Maud or the Madness was a better reading" (*"Prufrock* and *Maud:* From Plot to Symbol," in *Hateful Contraries* [Lexington, Ky., 1965], pp. 207–8*nn*). As my examination of *Maud* will show, I am in disagreement with Wimsatt, though I would not "make Tennyson the final interpreter of his own poem."

5. *Memoir,* p. 331.

6. *Past and Present,* Book I, ch. 1. George O. Marshall ("An Incident from Carlyle in Tennyson's 'Maud,'" *Notes & Queries,* n.s. 6, 204: 77–78) was the first to point out this source: "Mammonite" was almost surely suggested by Carlyle's chapter title "Gospel of Mammonism," Book III, ch. 11.

pel of Mammonism" (Book III, ch. II), Sauerteig, speaking of "the modern English soul," asks, " 'What *is* his Hell, after all these reputable, oft-repeated Hearsays, what is it? With hesitation, with astonishment, I pronounce it to be: The terror of "Not succeeding"; of not making money, fame, or some other figure in the world,—chiefly of not making money! Is not that a somewhat singular Hell?' " Moreover, modern English Hell is specifically related by Carlyle to Dante's Hell. In the "Midas" chapter, a tourist who had visited the workhouses concludes, "There was something that reminded me of Dante's Hell in the look of all this; and I rode swiftly away." It is also in this chapter that Carlyle relates "starveling Tom," the child of the Stockport mother and father, to "little Gaddo," the son of Ugolino of the *Inferno.* Tennyson certainly appears to have had *Past and Present* in mind at the beginning of *Maud* and therefore may well have had Dante in mind too. We also know that in the fall and winter of 1854, while Tennyson was working on *Maud,* he and his wife read the *Inferno* together.[7]

Perhaps it is not specious, therefore, to suggest that the opening of *Maud,* with its description of

> . . . the dreadful hollow behind the little wood
> Its lips in the field above are dabbled with blood-red
>   heath,
> The red-ribbed ledges drip with a silent horror of blood,
> And Echo there, whatever is asked her, answers 'Death.'
>
> (I, 1–4)

has a Dantesque quality and may have been associated in Tennyson's mind with the *Inferno,* in the same way that Carlyle associated the materialistic corruption of modern England with the *Inferno.* If such a suggestion is true, then there is reason to believe that the realistic opening of *Maud* may also be symbolic, that it need not be reduced to the topical concerns of the day but may be seen as a symbolic Hell, after the manner of Dante, from which the hero is able to emerge through his love for Maud.

Of course, the Hell which the hero inhabits is not only external but is an inward Hell also. Before Maud is actually introduced

7. *Memoir,* p. 319.

into the poem, the hero tells us he has "neither hope nor trust" (I, 30). From a Christian point of view he is guilty of the sin of despair and inhabits his own Hell. When by the end of the first section of Part I he has determined "I will bury myself in myself, and the Devil may pipe to his own" (I, 76), he is guilty of a serpent pride which Tennyson had so often dealt with in early poems: he is a morbid soul, not radically different from the soul of *The Palace of Art* or from Simeon Stylites, and in some ways similar to the mariners of *The Lotos-Eaters,* determined on withdrawal from society into self.[8] There is a touch of incipient madness, but substantial reason for his morbidity. Orphaned by villainy and made desperate by a ruthless and vicious age, the hero is driven to the edge of sanity. Unlike the hero of *Locksley Hall,* however, whose desperation is the result of frustrated adolescent love and whose conversion to a life of action is immediate and unmotivated, the hero of *Maud* undergoes a gradual regeneration from his state of credible morbidity through the quite believable agency of Maud. He is allowed, in other words, sufficient motivation for his initial plight and for the transformation which takes place in his character. His determination on a life of action at the end of the poem, diametrically opposed to his withdrawal at the beginning, is the perfectly credible and consistent result of the regenerative power of his love for Maud.

Maud is first seen by the hero in section II of Part I, and he describes her as "Perfectly beautiful" but "Dead perfection, no more; nothing more, if it had not been / For a chance of travel, a paleness, an hour's defect of the rose" (I, 80, 83–84). And he is hesitant about loving her: "And up in the high Hall-garden I see her pass like a light; / But sorrow seize me if ever that light be my leading star!" (I, 112–13). His hesitation is not the result of Maud's unworthiness, as the imagery suggests her worth, but of the hero's cynicism, a cynicism that makes him again determine on a life of withdrawal, which if less egotistical than his earlier determination to bury himself in himself is only slightly so:

> Be mine a philosopher's life in the quiet woodland ways,
> Where if I cannot be gay let a passionless peace be my lot,

8. An earlier version read, "I will bury myself in my books." See Ricks, *Poems,* p. 1046n.

> Far-off from the clamour of liars belied in the hubbub of
> lies;
> From the long-necked geese of the world that are ever
> hissing dispraise
> Because their natures are little, and, whether he heed it
> or not,
> Where each man walks with his head in a cloud of
> poisonous flies.   (I, 150–55)

The hero concludes this section with the determination to "flee from the cruel madness of love," finding Maud "unmeet for a wife" because she has "but fed on the roses and lain in the lilies of life" (I, 156, 158, 161).

From this section on, Maud's influence on the hero increases and the images which surround her are developed. Two of the dominant images used to describe Maud—the lily and the rose— are brought together in this section for the first time (though as we have seen she is earlier associated with the rose). John Killham is very likely right in his suggestion that Tennyson drew the images of the milkwhite faun (I, 158) and the roses and lilies from Andrew Marvell's *The Nymph Complaining for the Death of her Faun*.[9] (Of course, the symbolic values of the images, regardless of their sources, would be determined by the necessities of *Maud*.) E. D. H. Johnson argues that the images begin by symbolizing purity and passion, also love, and the rose at least develops variously as the poem moves toward its conclusion.[10] Wendell Stacy Johnson says of the images in the poem, "if the rose suggests violence, the lily symbolizes denial and, ultimately, death."[11]

There seems to be both agreement and disagreement on the part of critics—agreement that the lily and rose are important symbols, and disagreement as to what they symbolize. The dis-

9. "Tennyson's *Maud*—The Function of the Imagery," in Killham, *Critical Essays on the Poetry of Tennyson*, pp. 229–30. Killham sees in the English garden of *Maud* with its lilies and roses a "Persian-inspired" one, the result of Tennyson's reading in Persian literature. See *Tennyson and "The Princess,"* pp. 214, 215.

10. "The Lily and the Rose: Symbolic Meaning in Tennyson's *Maud*," *PMLA*, 64 (1949): 1222–27.

11. "The Theme of Marriage in Tennyson," *VN*, no. 12 (Autumn 1957): 7. See also Joseph, *Tennysonian Love*, p. 110: "In 'Maud' the lily represents the shrinking reticence of the lover and the rose his potential for aggressive passion, the two sides of his personality that he projects onto Maud."

agreement is perhaps no more than Tennyson expected and hoped for. In the "Moral" to an earlier poem, *The Day-Dream* (1842), the poet asks,

> And is there any moral shut
>   Within the bosom of the rose?
>
> But any man that walks the mead,
>   In bud or blade, or bloom, may find,
> According as his humours lead,
>   A meaning suited to his mind.
> And liberal applications lie
>   In Art like Nature, dearest friend;
> So 'twere to cramp its use, if I
>   Should hook it to some useful end.

I take this to mean that one is not amiss in Tennyson's poetry to seek a meaning or "moral," derivable from both Art and Nature, for such images as the rose. In *Maud,* while I do not deny that the lily and the rose may signify innocence and passion, I think there is another possibility overlooked by the critics. In *Balin and Balan,* published long after *Maud* (1885), Tennyson clarifies the meanings of the lily and the rose in *The Idylls of the King.* While Balin waits in a garden where a walk of roses is crossed by a walk of lilies, he overhears Sir Lancelot describe a dream:

> . . . . Last night methought I saw
> That maiden Saint who stands with lily in hand
> In yonder shrine. All round her prest the dark,
> And all the light upon her silver face
> Flowed from the spiritual lily that she held.   (255–59)

Guinevere answers: "'Sweeter to me' she said 'this garden rose / Deep-hued and many folded!'" (264–65). In the *Idylls* Guinevere rejects the "spiritual lily" and chooses the rose, as she chooses the flesh rather than the spirit. Lancelot also chooses flesh rather than spirit when he chooses Guinevere, the rose, rather than Elaine, "the lily maid of Astolat." As we shall see in a later chapter, in *The Idylls of the King,* at any rate, the lily and the rose represent quite clearly the spirit and the flesh.

I suggest that in *Maud* the lily and the rose have a similar symbolic value. Though Maud may represent for the hero a combination of innocence and passion, she is, as "Queen lily and rose in one," the combination of flesh and spirit. By identifying Maud with both the rose and the lily, Tennyson is insisting on her physical *and* spiritual reality, and such insistence is of considerable importance. For to deny either the flesh or the spirit is to lose the way to spiritual regeneration, because the only way to the spirit is through the flesh, as we saw in *In Memoriam*. As Carlyle had said in a slightly different context in *Past and Present*, "the Ideal always has to grow in the Real" (II, iv) .

*

The diction and imagery which surround Maud, in addition to the lily and the rose, provide us with the means to understanding her role in the hero's spiritual regeneration, in his ascent out of Hell. The language with which Maud is described has a religious flavor which suggests a beatification of her, a beatification which culminates in her return to the hero at the end of the poem from "the band of the blest." In her role in the hero's regeneration, it is perhaps not surprising that at times she shares the attributes of Beatrice; in addition, as the poem develops she is seen to share those attributes which we normally associate with Christ.

To begin with, Tennyson seems to insist on Maud's paleness, which the hero refers to four times in only ten lines (I, 84–93) . To insist that the paleness of Maud is analogous to the paleness of Beatrice, which for Dante seemed "the colour of Love," [12] would be to insist on more than can be proved, though such may have been the case. More importantly, the language with which the hero speaks of Maud in sections v and vi of Part I seems to go beyond the traditional hyperbole of secular love poetry. In those sections she is endowed by him with light and grace (I, 176) , and her voice promises a joy and a glory (I, 182, 183) , which if the hero cannot share he can at least fall at her feet and adore (I, 186–89) . When she touches his hand, she makes him *"divine* amends" (I, 202, italics mine) , and the glove which covers her hand is "sacred" (I, 274) . Perhaps this language only rather mildly sug-

---

12. See Charles Williams, *The Figure of Beatrice,* p. 42.

gests beatification, but as the influence of Maud on the hero increases, so do her divine attributes.

In section XIII of Part I we are told that

> Some peculiar mystic grace
> Made [Maud] only the child of her mother,
> And heaped the whole inherited sin
> On that huge scapegoat of the race,
> All, all upon the brother.   (I, 482–86)

Such is not the usual language of traditional secular love poetry
—to suggest that mystic grace allowed a kind of virgin birth, as it
were, to produce Maud. Dante, of course, says essentially the
same thing about Beatrice: quoting Homer he says, "From heaven
she had her birth, and not from mortal clay," or as Charles Williams translates, "She did not seem the daughter of a mortal
man, but of God."[13] Though Maud appears to be supernatural,
however, she remains at the same time, as does Beatrice, or Christ
for that matter, a physical reality.[14]

Maud also has other divine attributes. In section XVI of Part I
Maud's agency in the hero's salvation is suggested. The hero
speaks of

> . . . the grace that, bright and light as the crest
> Of a peacock, sits on her shining head,
> And she knows it not: O, if she knew it,
> To know her beauty might half undo it.
> I know it the one bright thing to save
> My yet young life in the wilds of Time,
> Perhaps from madness, perhaps from crime,
> Perhaps from a selfish grave.   (I, 552–59)

The suggestion seems to be that salvation is worked out in time
and that the means to that salvation is love. When the hero remarks that her beauty may save him from a "selfish grave," he
can perhaps be understood in many ways: first, she may prevent

---

13. *Vita Nuova*, p. 2; *The Figure of Beatrice*, p. 20.

14. Hallam, of course, insisted on the historical reality of both Beatrice
Portinari and Laura, denying to them exclusively allegorical roles in Dante and
Petrarch. See "On Gabriele Rossetti's Dante Theories," in *Hallam*, pp. 257, 265.

him from committing suicide; second, she may keep him from burying himself in himself as he had determined to do in the opening section; third, through love, which is selfless, one may avoid the grave, that is, overcome death in immortality—be "saved" in the theological sense. The imagery suggests that the beauty which can save him is not merely physical, but spiritual as well. The hero finds that grace sits on Maud's shining head like the crest of a peacock. In traditional Christian symbolism, the peacock is used to symbolize the many graces which endow the soul with beauty at the time of baptism.[15] If the hero is not clearly aware of the spiritual grace of Maud as a means of his spiritual salvation, the poet is apparently aware and has therefore chosen the images and diction of this section for both their literal and symbolic value, or perhaps for their natural as well as spiritual application.

Maud has thus far been described in the poem as divine; she is endowed with grace and the power to save; she is by implication perhaps the means to immortal life. She is the means through which the hero has "climbed nearer out of lonely Hell" (I, 678). In section xix of Part I she has perhaps, by implication again, the power of atonement: the hero asks,

> . . . do I dream of bliss?
> I have walked awake with Truth.
> O when did a morning shine
> So rich in atonement as this
> For my dark-dawning youth.   (I, 686–90)

I assume that the hero's "dream of delight" is of Maud. The hero means literally that Maud is true or real and not merely a dream and that her love has made the day so bright that it atones for the darkness of his youth. But the language seems somewhat strange. If he means Maud when he says he has walked with Truth, and if she is the means through which the morning atones for his dark youth, that youth sinfully selfish and associated with Hell, then he has attributed to her powers generally reserved to Christ alone. (There is indeed further evidence that Tennyson

15. Sister M. A. Knapp, *Christian Symbols* (Milwaukee, 1938), p. 147. The peacock is also a Persian image (see Killham, *Tennyson and "The Princess,"* p. 215), but its use here seems to me to be Christian.

associated Maud with Christ. The following two lines—382–83 —were deleted from section x of Part I of an earlier version by Tennyson: "And Maud, who when I had languished long, / Reached me a shining hand of help." If Christopher Ricks is right, and I think he is, that "The second MS line will have seemed too close to *In Memoriam* lxxxiv 43: 'Would reach us out the shining hand,'"[16] we may assume that Christ, whose shining hand is spoken of in the elegy, was not far from Tennyson's mind when he worked on *Maud*.)

In the concluding section of Part I, perhaps the most famous section of the poem, Maud is given a further divine power—the power to resurrect. The hero says in the concluding verse,

> She is coming, my own, my sweet;
>   Were it ever so airy a tread,
> My heart would hear her and beat,
>   Were it earth in an earthy bed;
> My dust would hear her and beat,
>   Had I lain for a century dead;
> Would start and tremble under her feet,
>   And blossom in purple and red.   (I, 916–23)

The imagery used here is the same used by Tennyson twenty-two years later in *Demeter and Persephone*. In that poem the fields of Enna have replaced "the valleys of Paradise" in *Maud* (line 893 of this section), though the two were closely related, as we have seen, in Tennyson's mind. In *Demeter and Persephone* there is a resurrection out of Hell into the light of the Sun:

> But when before have Gods or men beheld
> The Life that had descended re-arise,
> And lighted from above him by the Sun?   (29–31)[17]

16. Ricks, *Poems*, pp. 1059–60nn.

17. Maud is identified with the sun in a number of places in the poem, but specifically in verse ix of this section:

> Queen rose of the rosebud garden of girls,
>   Come hither, the dances are done,
> In gloss of satin and glimmer of pearls,
>   Queen lily and rose in one;
> Shine out, little head, sunning over with curls,
>   To the flowers, and be their sun.   (I, 902–7)

The myth of Persephone has been interpreted as anticipatory of the story of Christ,[18] and in the later poem Persephone seems to be identified with the God of Love. We are not, of course, justified in so identifying Maud because certain images are similar. And yet the conception of the hero's dust flowering at the touch of Maud's feet to "blossom in purple and red" is a striking one, and it is repeated in *Demeter and Persephone:*

> For, see, thy foot has touched it; all the space
> Of blank earth-baldness clothes itself afresh,
> And breaks into the crocus-purple hour
> That saw thee vanish.   (48–51)

The same image is used to express the same idea of rebirth. And very much the same image is used to express the same idea in the Prologue to *In Memoriam:*

> Thou madest Life in man and brute;
> Thou madest Death; and lo, thy foot
> Is on the skull which thou hast made.
>
> Thou wilt not leave us in the dust:
> Thou madest man, he knows not why,
> He thinks he was not made to die;
> And thou hast made him: thou art just.   (6–12)

In both *Demeter and Persephone* and *In Memoriam* there is hope for rebirth through the agency of one whose worship is Love. The similarity of the images in the three poems seems at least to reinforce the suggestion that Maud is at once the natural and spiritual agent whose love allows the hero a symbolic rebirth in this life and the hope of a spiritual rebirth in the next.

With section XXII ends Part I of the poem. The hero has been brought out of Hell into the light of the sun by Maud. Where he had been selfish, his love has made him selfless to the point where he "would die / To save from some slight shame one simple girl" (I, 642–43). His character has gone through a motivated and quite credible transformation.

*

18. See Stange, in Killham, *Critical Essays on the Poetry of Tennyson*, p. 149.

Part II recounts the hero's duel with Maud's brother, Maud's death, and the hero's madness, which is surely, like Lear's, his symbolic death, as he describes himself as dead: "Dead, long dead, / Long dead! / And my heart is a handful of dust" (II, 239–41). He even imagines himself as buried, but, as he had predicted at the end of Part I, Maud has the power to resurrect him, to cause his dust to "blossom in purple and red." That rebirth takes place in Part III.

Part III opens with early spring and the imagery of the third section of Part I is repeated. Though the poem begins in autumn, where "the flying gold of the ruined woodlands drove through the air" (I, 12), it almost immediately shifts to spring, with "The shining daffodil dead, and Orion low in his grave" (I, 101). Spring is a time of germination, but the hero's distraught mind at the beginning of the poem associates it only with death, with the dead daffodil and the grave of Orion. What the hero does not realize at this time is that birth comes through death. In Part III of the poem the same images are used but the tone is radically different, as the hero has been reborn from his symbolic death of madness. The time is again spring:

> My mood is changed, for it fell at a time of year
> When the face of night is fair on the dewy downs,
> And the shining daffodil dies, and the Charioteer
> And starry Gemini hang like glorious crowns
> Over Orion's grave low down in the west.   (III, 4–8)

The poem has in a way come full circle. Both the daffodil and Orion, which had died at the beginning of the poem, have been reborn to die with the promise to be reborn again, and the hero, who begins in cynicism, ends in hope.

That the hero has been reborn into a new life at the end of the poem is generally admitted. The nature of that new life, however, has been generally misunderstood, and that misunderstanding is the result of identifying the war to which the hero dedicates his life with the Crimean debacle. Certainly the poem can be read to suggest approval of the Crimean War if it is read as a topical poem, and it is difficult to avoid identifying the "broad-brimmed hawker of holy things" (I, 370) with the war's most outspoken adversary, John Bright, in spite of Tennyson's protestations to the contrary.

For his approval of the Crimean War at its inception Tennyson can perhaps be forgiven, as he was apparently the typical Englishman in this regard.[19] If, on the other hand, Tennyson had bent the poem to fit a purely topical and propagandistic end, he should not be so easily forgiven. And yet he has not, I think, sacrificed the integrity of *Maud* to any propagandistic purpose. What the hero dedicates himself to at the end of the poem is warring for the good, and the principle of warring for the good in the poem transcends specific application.[20] What the hero does is enroll himself on the side of the warrior saints, who war in this life for the good. Imagery of war has been widely used to describe the struggle against evil and was of course used even by St. Paul (Eph. 6:11–17). Indeed in *The Victory of Faith* Julius Hare recommends the contemporary appeal of St. Paul's exhortation to fight the universal war against evil: "In each warfare Faith is to be your weapon,—your shield, as St. Paul terms it, to defend you against Sin, when it assails you with any of its poisoned arrows,—your sword, to fight against Sin in the world, when it has been so far brought into subjection within you, that you may aspire to be enrolled in the army which God sends forth to wage His battles against evil. Do not invert the rightful order. Do not fancy that you can work any good in the world, until the Evil Spirit has been cast out of your own hearts. Else your very best acts will be marred by selfishness: your virtues will only be splendid vices. Strive therefore in the first place to cast out the Evil Spirit

19. See, for example, Asa Briggs, *Victorian People* (New York and Evanston, 1955), p. 55: "The roots of Russophobia in England lay deeper than the revolutions of 1848. Between 1815 and 1830, writers like Sir Robert Wilson and George de Lacy Evans had argued that the Russian objective was Constantinople and that, once Constantinople was captured, universal dominion lay within Russia's 'easy grasp.' . . . Nothing fundamentally new was said by pamphleteers about Russia in 1854 and 1855 which had not been said by 1830. But, between 1848 and 1854, Russophobes stirred not limited sections of the reading public but large crowds of people." Cf. Tennyson's Russophobia in verses dated 1831–33 in Donahue, "Tennyson's 'Hail Briton!' and 'Tithon,' " p. 392.

20. Allan Danzig is surely the exception rather than the rule in his interpretation of the ending of *Maud:* "Tennyson, it is safe to say, is rarely, and certainly not here [in *Maud*], concerned with war at all" ("The Contraries: A Central Concept in Tennyson's Poetry," *PMLA*, 77 [1962]: 584).

from your own hearts." [21] The hero of *Maud*, I submit, has cast out the evil spirit of selfishness and now aspires "to be enrolled in the army which God sends forth to wage His battles against evil."

There are many indications in Part III of *Maud* that the war is a spiritual one against wickedness. For example, Maud returns to the hero in a dream "from a band of the blest," suggesting that she is, like Beatrice, in Paradise. After she speaks "of a hope for the world in the coming wars," she says,

> 'And in that hope, dear soul, let trouble have rest,
> Knowing I tarry for thee,' and pointed to Mars
> As he glowed like a ruddy shield on the Lion's breast.
>
> (III, 12–14)

This could mean, of course, that the British Lion is to wear the shield of Mars, the God of War, that is, that England should go to war against Russia in the Crimea. Maud may also be talking about the planet Mars in the constellation Leo. If Tennyson conceives of Maud as a kind of Beatrician figure, as I contend, we may perhaps legitimately associate the imagery here with the sphere of Mars, the sphere of the soldier saints, of Canto XVIII of the *Paradise;* as Beatrice points out to Dante the sphere of Mars, so perhaps does Maud to the hero.[22]

In the third section of Part III the hero says,

> And I stood on a giant deck and mixed my breath
> With a loyal people shouting a battle cry,
> Till I saw the dreary phantom arise and fly
> Far into the North, and battle, and seas of death.
>
> (III, 34–37)

21. P. 235. Hare uses the same image in *Guesses at Truth: Second Series*, p. 281: *"Be ye perfect, even as your Father in heaven is perfect.* This is the angel-trumpet which summons man to the warfare of duty." I use Hare here only as illustration of a pervasive Christian tradition viable for the Victorians, and not because I wish to demonstrate any specific indebtedness on Tennyson's part to Hare. Tennyson may have recalled St. Paul, as during the composition of *Maud* he had as a houseguest Benjamin Jowett, who was at the time preparing an edition of the Epistles of St. Paul (though he did not apparently include Ephesians in his edition).

22. Tennyson seems to have had the constellation in mind. Ricks glosses the line with the following note: "T. wrote 17 March 1854 (*Trinity College*): 'A boy was born last night—a stout little fellow. Mars was culminating in the Lion—does that mean soldiership?' The Lion represents Britain" (*Poems*, p. 1091n).

Surely E. K. Brown is wrong when he identifies the "dreary phantom" as Maud.[23] Maud, who has just come to him from the band of the blest "like a silent lightning under the stars" (9), could hardly have become so abruptly a "dreary phantom." It is much more likely that the dreary phantom which flies far into the North represents the forces of evil.[24] There is, of course, an extensive tradition which associates Satan with the North, a tradition which Milton follows in *Paradise Lost*.[25] Tennyson was certainly aware of this tradition, as he refers to the Red Knight in *The Last Tournament* (1871) as "like Satan in the North" (98).

Finally, the last lines of the poem, added by Tennyson after the first edition, evidently in an effort to clarify the spiritual nature of the warfare,[26] indicate that the hero at least believes that he is doing God's will: "I am one with my kind,/I embrace the purpose of God, and the doom assigned." What the hero had ignorantly predicted early in the poem, "I have not made the world, and He that made it will guide" (I, 149), has come true. God has indeed guided him through the agency of Maud, just as Dante had been guided through the agencies of Virgil and Beatrice. That the hero's spiritual development in the poem

---

23. "Dreary phantom: Maud, symbol here of the speaker's mental disease. In his new enthusiasm, old delusions fade from his mind" (*Victorian Poetry*, p. 758).

24. It is likely that Tennyson may have had the Czar in mind as a manifestation of the forces of evil.

25. Satan says,

> 'And all who under me thir Banners wave,
> Homeward with flying march where we possess
> The Quarters of the North.' (V, 687–89)

I have used Merritt Hughes' edition (New York, 1962). See also Hughes' note on the tradition behind Satan's quartering in the North, p. 132.

26. As *Maud* was received with "almost universal reprobation" (see Sir Charles Tennyson, *Tennyson*, pp. 285–92, for *Maud's* reception), Tennyson may have added the ending to clarify his position and defend himself against charges of warmongering. Ricks (*Poems*, p. 1092n) has the following note for the final six lines of the poem: "*1856; not 1855.* A British Museum copy of *1855* (first American edition) has cancelled drafts of this last stanza, which show T. attempting to relate the war to the love for Maud:

> Let it go or stay, so I walk henceforth resigned
> By the light of a love not lost, with a purer mind
> And rejoice in my native land, and am one with my kind.

Also: 'And I rise from a life half-lost with a better mind. . . .'"

should cause him to repudiate withdrawal into self and to dedicate himself to an active life is no more than one might expect
from Tennyson. We have seen that he occupied himself again and
again with such a theme. And, as Allan Danzig has pointed out,
the hero's final realization that he is one with his kind echoes a
similar realization on the part of the persona in *In Memoriam*.[27]
Maud, as a poem about spiritual regeneration ending in a dedication to an active life, is in a very real sense "the antiphonal voice
to 'In Memoriam.'"

*

Materials so ineffectually handled in *The Gardener's Daughter*, *Edwin Morris*, and *Locksley Hall* coalesce and are transformed in *Maud*. Without the sentimentality of the English
Idyls or the counterfeit emotions of *Locksley Hall*, *Maud* succeeds
where the earlier poems fail. It succeeds in part because it is sufficiently dramatic: the hero is so well realized—so consistent and
so convincingly motivated—that we are willing to see the world
through his eyes and accept it as his sight. We can sufficiently
suspend our disbelief in order to believe that Maud is for the hero
as she appears in the poem, as we can believe Beatrice to be as
she appears to Dante. Unlike Rose or Letty Hill or Cousin Amy,
whom we do not know at all, we know Maud as the hero does
and believe her to be what he tells us she is. The hero is so
consistent and credible that the poem, which is made up entirely
of his thoughts, is consistent and credible. Moreover, unlike the
three earlier poems, it is complete. The action of which it is an
imitation has a beginning, a middle, and an end.

Finally, those critics who speak of a gratuitous "jingo theme"
in *Maud*, who assume the Crimean War and judge the hero's
dedication to it as "hardly more than a sop to Victorian senti-

---

27. Danzig says of "I am one with my kind": "In this he [the hero] echoes the
speaker of *In Memoriam:* 'The shade by which my life was crost, / Which makes a
desert in the mind, / Has made me kindly with my kind' (LXVI), and 'I will not
shut me from my kind' (CVIII). But *In Memoriam*, arriving at a conclusion so
similar to that of *Maud*, traces an altogether different path. This fact serves to
reinforce the claim that the Crimean War has no essential meaning for the latter
poem" ("The Contraries: A Central Concept in Tennyson's Poetry," p. 585n) .

mentalism,"[28] could not arrive at such conclusions without previous biographical knowledge, and their judgments seem therefore prescriptive. Also those critics who wish to make the maddened lover in *Maud* a reflection of Tennyson himself[29] seem to me to ignore the art of the poem. To read the poem as a topical one or to read it as autobiography seems to me to reduce it to less than it is. The poem is an amazing achievement—a combination of lyric, dramatic, and narrative art—which of its kind has no rival in the language.

28. Johnson, *Alien Vision,* p. 31.

29. See, for example, Rader, *Tennyson's* Maud; Paden, *Tennyson in Egypt,* pp. 92–94; Arthur J. Carr, "Tennyson as a Modern Poet," in Killham, *Critical Essays on the Poetry of Tennyson,* p. 47n; and Joseph, *Tennysonian Love,* pp. 102–16.

5. *Idylls of the King:* A Prelude

EFORE we turn to an examination of the *Idylls of the King,* there are some preliminary considerations which should be taken care of. There are first the rather strange method of composition of the books of the *Idylls* and Tennyson's defense of their subject matter. There is second what I think to be the intellectual background out of which the *Idylls* comes. And there is third the overall structure of the poem.

*

First, the method of composition: the *Morte d'Arthur* was the earliest of the books, a first draft appearing in J. M. Heath's Commonplace Book with the earliest stanzas of *In Memoriam* in 1833.[1] It was not then published until *Poems* (1842), where the 270 lines (later incorporated into *The Passing of Arthur* with the omission of only one line[2]) were surrounded by a "frame" in defense of Arthurian romance. All was published under the title *The Epic.* In 1859, under the title of *Idylls of the King,* appeared four tales: *Enid, Vivien, Elaine,* and *Guinevere.* In 1869 four more *Idylls* appeared: *The Coming of Arthur, The Holy Grail, Pelleas and Ettare,* and *The Passing of Arthur.* Two more, *The Last Tournament* and *Gareth and Lynette,* were published in 1872 (*The Last Tournament* had appeared in *Contemporary Review* in 1871), and in 1885 the last of the *Idylls, Balin and Balan* (written in 1872), appeared in *Tiresias and Other Poems.* In 1873 *Enid,* then entitled *Geraint and Enid,* was divided

---

1. See *Memoir,* p. 92.

2. The 270 lines incorporated into *The Passing of Arthur* begin there with line 170 and run through line 440. The omitted line was "Sir Bedivere, the last of all his knights."

into two parts and in 1886 these two parts became *The Marriage of Geraint* and *Geraint and Enid.*

This rather odd mode of composition and publication, which spans a period of some fifty-five years, may seem to cast suspicion on the integrity of the *Idylls* in its final form. And yet Tennyson's lifelong concern with Arthurian legend[3] allows for the possibility, at least, of a unity beyond the loosely seasonal structure, the central character of Arthur, and Tennyson's rather vague thematic description of "Sense at war with Soul." The method of composition, in other words, need not necessarily argue against a general plan or conception which the poet may have entertained from the first and which would allow for a greater degree of unity than has generally been accorded the poem.

A second consideration is Tennyson's defense of his subject matter. Certainly Tennyson was aware that in retelling a medieval romance he might open himself to a charge of irrelevance and neglect of poetic responsibility. To avoid this charge he surrounded his earliest idyll, *Morte d'Arthur,* with an introduction and conclusion, amounting to some eighty-two lines, in *The Epic* of 1842.[4] It is in this "frame" that the poet, Everard Hall, is charged with having burnt "His epic, his King Arthur, some twelve books" (28) because "He thought that nothing new was said, or else / Something so said 'twas nothing—that a truth / Looks freshest in the fashion of the day" (30–32). And Hall agrees:

> 'Why take the style of those heroic times?
> For nature brings not back the Mastodon,
> Nor we those times; and why should any man
> Remodel models? these twelve books of mine
> Were faint Homeric echoes, nothing-worth,
> Mere chaff and draff, much better burnt. . . .' (35–40)

The speaker of the poem, after the recitation of the *Morte d'Arthur,* weakly defends its modernity: "Perhaps some modern

3. See Hallam Tennyson's discussion of this concern in *Memoir,* ch. xxviii.

4. That Tennyson is defending himself is clear from Fitzgerald's letter, quoted in *Memoir,* p. 162: "The 'Morte d'Arthur' when read to us from manuscript in 1835 had no introduction or epilogue; which was added to anticipate or excuse the 'faint Homeric echoes,' etc. (as in the 'Day-Dream'), to give a reason for telling an old-world tale." Tennyson was surely aware of Arnold's later defense in the "Preface" to the *Poems* (1853) against similar charges.

touches here and there / Redeemed it from the charge of nothing-ness" (278–79), and upon retirement he dreams that "King Arthur, like a modern gentleman" is "come again, and thrice as fair" (294, 298).

This, then, was Tennyson's defense, but the defense was not strong enough to withstand the attack of critics, most notably John Sterling, a fellow Apostle. Sterling wrote in the *Quarterly*, "The miraculous legend of 'Excalibar,' does not come very near to us, and as reproduced by any modern writer must be a mere ingenious exercise of fancy." [5] Edgar Shannon suggests that Sterling's criticism "apparently convinced Tennyson that an Arthurian epic could have no hope of critical or even general approval. Perhaps, as well, he was persuaded that it would be a retreat from his poetic duty." [6]

At any rate, years later Hallam Tennyson still felt the necessity to defend his father's modernization of Arthurian material: "he has made the old legends his own, restored the idealism, and infused into them a spirit of modern thought and an ethical significance, setting his characters in a rich and varied landscape; as indeed otherwise these archaic stories would not have appealed to the modern world at large." [7] Clearly, the charge of irrelevance against old tales kept Tennyson uncomfortable to the end. In 1889 he said, not of Arthurian legend this time, but of Greek myth: "I will write it [*Demeter and Persephone*], but when I write an antique like this I must put it into a frame—something modern about it. It is no use giving a mere *réchauffé* of old legends." [8]

Aware of the charges to which he was liable, Tennyson still completed the *Idylls,* apparently finding the tales both relevant and modern. One is led to ask how they are so. If they are not "a mere *réchauffé* of old legends," in what sense are they modern, for they have no modern frame around them? Hallam Tennyson's assertion that his father "restored the idealism, and infused

---

5. Quoted in Shannon, *Tennyson and the Reviewers*, p. 91. Sterling's article is reprinted in its entirety in John D. Jump, *Tennyson: The Critical Heritage*, pp. 103–25.

6. *Tennyson and the Reviewers*, p. 92.

7. *Memoir*, p. 518. One feels that Sterling would have found such a vague defense less than satisfactory.

8. *Memoir*, p. 724.

into them a spirit of modern thought and an ethical significance"
suggests a process of dressing new ideas in old clothes or perhaps
placing modern ideas in a kind of timeless setting. It is this kind
of process which John Killham suggests that Tennyson employed
in *The Princess.* In that poem, Killham says, the poet "is concerned to follow the counsel he gave Emily Sellwood in 1839—
'Annihilate within yourself these two dreams of Space and Time.'
Contemporary events are not to be viewed solely in their temporal context; they can be seen to contain within themselves
hints and suggestions of wider import, and these the poet can
elucidate by placing them in quite different settings, settings
of a timeless kind like those to be found in romance and folk-
tale. Only when dissociated from 'modernity' can the true significance of modern movements be grasped clearly." [9] Killham is very
probably right that it was such a process which Tennyson employed in *The Princess.* It is a process of infusion, a process of
pouring new wine into old bottles. But it is not, I think, the process employed in *Idylls of the King.*

Tennyson does not in the *Idylls* infuse an archaic setting with
modern ideas; he extracts from the Arthurian world what he
thinks relevant to the modern world. He does what Charles
Kingsley had praised him for doing in 1849: "We can trust *him*
[Tennyson] with the Past, for he has discovered the great historic
secret of finding the Present in the Past, and embodying in out-
wardly obsolete legends eternal truths which shall stand good to
the end of time." [10] Whether or not he succeeded in embodying the
truths which he found, one can credit Tennyson in the *Idylls of
the King* with being in a very real sense "historical." [11] He was

9. *Tennyson and "The Princess,"* p. 64.
10. "Recent Poetry, and Recent Verse," *Fraser's Magazine,* 39 (1849) : 570.
11. It can be argued, of course, that Arthurian legend is myth, not history,
but the distinction is not of as great moment as it might seem. As Julius Hare
pointed out, "Thucydides, true and profound as he is, cannot be truer or pro-
founder than his contemporary, Sophocles" (*Guesses at Truth: First Series,* p. 218).
Poetry and myth are as true as history. Indeed, Milman, for example, saw the
Middle Ages as "a mythic period, when poetry and history [were] inseparable"
(Forbes, *The Liberal Anglican Idea of History,* p. 81). For Tennyson, I imagine,
to separate myth from history would have been to search for fact, not truth. Paden
distinguishes between two Arthurs, "one a semi-historical British leader of the
sixth century, the other a mythological figure." For his discussion of the Arthur of
Helio-Arkite mystery, see *Tennyson in Egypt,* pp. 75 ff. I am, of course, in disagree-

quite as much concerned and in a similar way concerned with theories of history as Carlyle was. He could devote his poetic energies to Arthurian legend for precisely the same reasons that Carlyle could devote his energies to *Past and Present*. It will be remembered, for example, that the entire second book of *Past and Present* describes life in a twelfth-century monastery, "in the hope," Carlyle says, "of perhaps illustrating our own poor Century thereby." Indeed, as the title suggests, the whole work is concerned with delineating the relationship between past and present. Because "the Centuries . . . are all lineal children of one another" and because "often, in the portrait of early grandfathers, this and the other enigmatic feature of the newest grandson shall disclose itself, to mutual elucidation" (Book II, Ch. 1), Carlyle clearly hopes to be exonerated from charges of archaism and irrelevance. And, it can be argued, the world of Arthur's Round Table is no more archaic or irrelevant than the world of Abbot Samson and Jocelin of Brakelond. On the contrary, the *Idylls,* dealing as it does with a whole cycle of national history, is on a grander scale, but hardly less pertinent, than Carlyle's treatment of the microcosmic monastery of St. Edmundsbury. Moreover, the historicism of the *Idylls* is modern, because the theories of history upon which it seems to be based accord with the theories espoused by the most modern historians of Tennyson's day—the Liberal Anglicans.[12]

*

In Chapter 2, I suggested the correlation between Liberal Anglican thinking and the thought of *In Memoriam*. There Tennyson was concerned with the spiritual advance of the individual. In *Maud* the individual was again the poet's major concern, though the rejection of a decadent society at the beginning

ment with Robert Preyer ("Alfred Tennyson: The Poetry and Politics of Conservative Vision," *VS*, 9 [1966]: 335), who suggests that Tennyson "was far more concerned with theories of evolution than with theories of history."

12. Such a developmental theory of social growth and decay is also common to Saint-Simonism, a doctrine with which Tennyson was familiar at least as early as 1832 and to which Carlyle was clearly indebted; see Killham, *Tennyson and "The Princess,"* pp. 37–38. Hare also mentions the Saint Simonians when discussing the German conception of history; see *Guesses at Truth: Second Series,* p. 272.

of the poem and the acceptance of a socially significant role by
the spiritually regenerated hero at the end of the poem mark
a shift in perspective. In the *Idylls of the King* Tennyson's vision
expands further from the individual world to the world of the nation, from the natural world to the social one.

In Memoriam, if it was indebted to the Liberal Anglicans,
seems to me to have been indebted to them as theologians; that
is, the idea of a permanent and unified spiritual world manifesting itself in change and diversity, the eternal presence of Christ,
the necessity of approaching the spiritual through the natural,
and the role of love in spiritual growth were variously held Liberal Anglican theological theories apparently shared by Tennyson. In *Idylls of the King* Tennyson seems, if indebted, to be
indebted to the Liberal Anglicans as historians rather than as
theologians, though their theology was never divorced from history. The Liberal Anglican science of history, which sought to
apply the lessons of national history to contemporary social problems, and their philosophy of history, which attempted to trace
the spiritual advance of mankind in universal history, both seem
to me to be reflected in the *Idylls.* A recognition of them can
help clarify some apparent confusions about the poem.

First there is the science of history. Lawrence Poston III
rightly observes, "It is surely no very original observation to say
that throughout the *Idylls* Tennyson often draws an analogy between individual and state." [13] Though such an analogy is probably as old as history, it is the dominant one in the Liberal Anglican discussion of the development of nations, the laws of which
the science of history sought to discover. As Julius Hare put it in
Guesses at Truth, "The natural life of nations, as well as of individuals, has its fixed course and term. It springs forth, grows
up, reaches its maturity, decays, perishes." [14] Thomas Arnold saw
the relationship between the individual and the state in the same
light: "Arnold's theory of the social progress of states starts from
the analogy between the life-course of the nation and that of the

13. "The Argument of the Geraint-Enid Books in *Idylls of the King*," *VP,*
2 (1964): 275.
14. *Second Series,* p. 248. See also p. 272, where Hare compares the individual
to history as microcosm to macrocosm and remarks the development of the idea in
Germany.

individual, part of the Romantic background to Niebuhr and the historical school of law. . . . The course of a nation's history . . . resembled the life of an individual, or a plant, or the astronomical progress of a day or a year. It had its boyhood and manhood, its intermediate stages and transition periods, its dawn, high-noon and dusk, its spring, summer, autumn and winter, its blossom and seed time." [15] The metaphors multiply, but the idea is the same: nations are born, grow, and die with the inevitability or at least the universality of other natural phenomena. They, like individuals, are subject to laws of generation and degeneration and the cycles of national history find their analogies in the cyclical processes of nature. Not only are the nations themselves subject to superannuation and decay, but the institutions and ideals which they affirm are likewise so subject. Carlyle in *Past and Present* is in agreement with the Liberal Anglicans: "By the law of Nature, too, all manner of Ideals have their fatal limits and lot; their appointed periods, of youth, of maturity or perfection, of decline, degradation, and final death and disappearance. There is nothing born but has to die" (Book II, Ch. IV). Such a developmental theory of history is, of course, rather easily adapted to nineteenth-century evolutionary theory, but without a corollary philosophy of history it becomes depressingly fatalistic. [16]

The Liberal Anglican philosophy of history concerned itself not with the cyclical history of nations, of institutions, or of ideals, but with the more or less linear movement of universal history, not with natural process but with spiritual progress. As we saw in Chapter 2, the Liberal Anglicans distinguished two kinds of "progress": the "progress" discernible in the growth of nations,

15. Forbes, *The Liberal Anglican Idea of History*, p. 20. Buckley associates the seasonal metaphor in the *Idylls* with Spengler: "The seasonal symbolism foreshadows the 'natural' metaphor used by Spengler in his theory of rising and falling civilizations. As Reinhold Niebuhr paraphrases Spengler, 'All civilizations pass through ages analogous to spring, summer, autumn and winter; which is to say that historical organisms are equated with natural ones.' But, says Niebuhr, this means that the freedom of history is illusory and that all moves by necessity. . . . Despite the metaphor, however, Tennyson is much closer to Toynbee than to Spengler, insofar as he believes that civilizations are free to make mistakes" (*Tennyson*, p. 281n4).

16. Niebuhr, who was unable to reconcile the developmental theory of the history of nations with any belief in the idea of progress, died, we are told, "in an atmosphere of unrelieved pessimism" (Forbes, *The Liberal Anglican Idea of History*, p. 19).

a progress which is cyclical and natural, and "true progress" which is "a gradual advance, through the childhood-manhood rhythm of nations, towards the final goal of God's purpose which it is not given us to see." [17] "True progress" is neither cyclical nor natural, but linear and spiritual. National history, in other words, records natural process; universal history records true progress.

If we can assume for the moment that Tennyson regarded history similarly, his choice of Arthurian history seems reasonable. Arthur's kingdom being both English and Christian would have been appropriate to Tennyson's audience. Moreover, because "each national cycle is a complete example of development, and the stages of this development form 'analogous periods' comparable to similar stages in the development of other nations," [18] the Arthurian cycle could illuminate Victorian England. But in order to do so, the cycle had necessarily to be historical; that is, Tennyson could not have used a contemporary national cycle. If at least part of the burden of *Idylls of the King* is the generation, growth, and decay of a nation, the poet would have to deal with a nation which had gone through the whole cycle; that is, he would necessarily have dealt with the past, where the cycle was complete, rather than the present, where the nation was in the process of the cycle and the destruction could only be speculative. And so to teach the lessons of history, both the scientific lesson of national history and the philosophical lesson of universal history, Tennyson of necessity chose a historical period.

If we can assume two separable but corollary conceptions of history in operation in *Idylls of the King*, we will perhaps have the means for clarifying the point of greatest controversy about the poem—the assignment of responsibility in the destruction of the kingdom. Stanley J. Solomon can be taken to represent one side of the argument: "There is extensive textual evidence to support my view that the one sin [of Lancelot and Guinevere] determines the calamity of the kingdom." [19] F. E. L. Priestley can·

17. Ibid., p. 65.
18. Ibid., p. 43.
19. "Tennyson's Paradoxical King," *VP*, 1 (1963): 264*n*. See also Johnson, *The Alien Vision*, p. 43: "The adulterous passion of the Queen and Lancelot . . . becomes the principal agency for the downfall of Arthur's chivalric order"; and Pitt, *Tennyson Laureate*, p. 187: "The Table was destroyed by the adultery of Guinevere and Lancelot."

represent the other: "The defection of Guinevere is by no means the sole, or perhaps the chief, cause of the failure of Arthur's plans."[20] Arthur himself suggests a quite different "cause" for the destruction of the kingdom. Arthur's final judgment, and perhaps the final judgment of the poem, which is given us in *The Passing of Arthur* (retained entire from the *Morte d'Arthur*), is that " 'The old order changeth, yielding place to new, / And God fulfils himself in many ways, / Lest one good custom should corrupt the world' " (408–10). Such a conclusion seems clearly to demonstrate that, in Arthur's mind at least, the destruction of the kingdom is both inevitable and providential.

If the destruction of Arthur's kingdom is inevitable, as the science of history demonstrates the destruction of all nations to be, and as the poem seems to conclude, then the exercise of moral choice, on the part of Guinevere or of anyone else, seems irrelevant. And yet, such is not the case. It is true that the individual cannot prevent social disintegration—even the ideal individual like Arthur. It is also true that no nation can perfect itself, that is, reform itself to the degree that change is unnecessary. But because the nation is doomed, as all nations are doomed, at its inception, it does not follow that there is no necessity for moral choice, that determinism rules all. A nation can, through the exercise of moral choice, either contribute to the spiritual advance of mankind, or it can stagnate or retrogress. Therefore, on the proper exercise of moral choice depends "true progress," the progress of universal history. Though the nation itself may decay, it has the opportunity to take a step forward in universal history, to play a positive part in the fulfillment of God's providential plan. Arthur's kingdom has advanced through the virtue of the Round Table over its predecessors and has therefore succeeded, though it has not perfected itself, as progress does not mean perfectibility.[21] Both the impossibility of perfection and the necessity to attempt it in the natural world are suggested by the old seer, who tells Gareth, "the King / Will bind thee by such vows, as

20. "Tennyson's *Idylls*," in Killham, *Critical Essays on the Poetry of Tennyson,* p. 243. See also Clyde Ryals, *From the Great Deep* (Athens, Ohio, 1967), p. 77: "Lancelot's and Guinevere's sin is . . . I believe, not the cause but the symptom of what is wrong in Camelot."

21. For Hare's rejection of the possibility of perfectibility, see *Guesses at Truth: Second Series,* pp. 252–73.

is a shame / A man should not be bound by, yet the which / No man can keep" (265–68). Not only is Arthur's kingdom in advance of its predecessor, Rome, now grown too weak to drive the heathen from her wall, but it is in advance of its morally weak contemporaries—the kingdom of Pellam, which has stagnated and resembles an idolatrous Rome, and the kingdom of Mark, which has retrogressed, has returned to the bestial life before Arthur's advent.

Furthermore, when a nation decays, what comes to destruction is the shadow, not the reality. The spiritual is the real. This it seems to me is the point of the old seer's remark to Gareth as he is about to enter the city, "For there is nothing in it as it seems / Saving the King; though some there be that hold / The King a shadow, and the city real" (260–62). Quite clearly those who hold the King a shadow and the city real are mistaken, as the city comes to destruction, but the King passes to Avilion with the promise to come again. The natural, the shadow, goes through its destined cycle, but the spiritual, the reality, is permanent. It must have been some such understanding of spiritual progress in the face of natural decay, of two separable conceptions of history more or less clearly apprehended, which prompted Hallam Tennyson's judgment of the *Idylls:* "Yet in spite of the ebbs and flows in the tide of human affairs, in spite of the temporary bearing down of the pure and lofty purpose, the author has carefully shadowed forth the spiritual progress and advance of the world, and has enshrined man's highest hopes in this new-old legend, crowning with a poet's prophetic vision the vague and disjointed dreams of a bygone age." [22] At any rate, the two conceptions of history speculated upon by the Liberal Anglicans are a means of reconciling apparent antinomies in *Idylls of the King.* Lancelot, Guinevere, and others are morally culpable at the same time that their purity would not have prevented the destruction of the kingdom; though they could not prevent social disintegration, their sinfulness affects both their individual spiritual advancement and the degree of spiritual advancement Arthur's kingdom is able to make over its predecessors.

*

22. *Memoir,* p. 524.

Natural analogies for the cyclical progress of nations—analogies to the progress of the astronomical day or year or to the life of the individual—provide singularly appropriate structuring devices for a poem like *Idylls of the King*. For example, readers of the poem have long been aware of its loosely seasonal structure, which, in the first two idylls, opens in spring with the marriage of Arthur in May and the coming of Gareth to Arthur's court after Easterday. It then moves in the middle idylls through summer to the autumn of *The Last Tournament,* to the apparent winter of *Guinevere,* and to the advent of the new year in the final line of *The Passing of Arthur*. I say that the seasonal structure is a loose one because the twelve books of the poem are not equated to the twelve months of the year, nor is innocence the unequivocal property of spring and summer and guilt of autumn and winter.[23] It should be noted, for example, that as the seeds of spring carry within them the germ of decay of winter, so is the promise of fruition in the kingdom which Gareth represents accompanied by the shadow of corruption. Gareth is guilty, with whatever laudable cause, of the lie, the sin which contributes to the destruction of the kingdom. And for all his virtue, he is the son of Lot and the brother of Gawain and Mordred. There is indeed the cycle of the year, but it is perhaps not so much the temporal year as it is what Julius Hare called the "moral year": "When we call to remembrance, however, that the course of time is marked, not by the rectilinear flight, but by the oscillations and pulsations of life, that life does not flow in a straight conspicuous stream into its ocean-home, but sinks sooner or later into the subterraneous caverns of death, that light does not keep on brightening into a more intense effulgence, but, in compassion to the infirmity of our organs, allows them to bathe ever and anon and seek refreshment in darkness, that the moral year, like the natural, is not one continued spring and summer, but has its seasons of decay, during which new growths are preparing, that the ways of Providence in this world, as crossed and interrupted by the self-will of man, are not solely from good to better, but

23. Herbert Marshall McLuhan suggests that "The twelve idylls follow the cycle of the zodiac, each book corresponding faithfully to the traditional character of the twelve 'houses' of the zodiac" (Introduction to *Alfred Lord Tennyson: Selected Poetry* [New York, 1964], p. xix) .

often, in a merciful condescension to our frailty, through evil to good, we shall understand that a more advanced stage of civilization does not necessarily imply a better state of society, least of all in any one particular country; which, it is possible, may already have played out its part, and be doomed to fall, while others rise up in its stead." [24]

Tennyson also employs as a structural device the cycle of the individual life. The birth and death of the nation finds an analogue in the birth and death of its King. But more than that, the pattern of maturation through which both the individual and the nation move from infancy through youth to maturity reverses itself so that the pattern of degeneration is its exact opposite—from maturity to youth to infancy. In the *Idylls* the Arthurian kingdom begins in infancy with the birth of Arthur; it then proceeds through the youth of Gareth to the maturity of Geraint. When it traces its inevitable retrogression after the death of Elaine and the disastrous pursuit of the grail, it does so by taking a youth, Pelleas, who is exactly like Gareth, and delineating his degeneration as the reversal of Gareth's development. The progress of the nation has been arrested and its retrogression has begun; it is therefore appropriate that the tournament at which Pelleas wins the circlet for the degenerate Ettare is the "Tournament of Youth." The last tournament of the next book of the *Idylls* is appropriately a further inevitable step toward dissolution—"The Tournament of the Dead Innocence." It is a tournament to commemorate the death of the infant "Nestling." The cyclical pattern from birth through infancy and youth to maturity and its reversal from maturity through youth and infancy to death is a pattern followed by humans and nations alike.

As we have seen, natural cycles of various kinds—seasonal, diurnal, astronomical, or cycles of human life—consistently provided the analogies with which the Liberal Anglicans described the generation and degeneration of nations. If indeed Tennyson

24. *Guesses at Truth: Second Series*, p. 275. Cf. also p. 270: "In a word, the purpose and end of the history of the world is to realize the idea of humanity. All the while too, as in the outward world there is a mutual adaptation and correspondence between the course of the seasons, and the fruits they are to mature, so may we feel assured that, at every stage in the progress of history, such light and warmth will be vouchsafed to mankind from above, as they may be able to bear, and as their temporary needs may require."

is concerned in the *Idylls* with the science of history, apposite structuring devices were certainly near at hand.

In addition to the cyclical patterns employed by Tennyson there are what might be called circular patterns. For example, though the *Idylls* completes the cycle from birth to death, in many ways it can be said to inscribe a circle and end where it began. Arthur for instance dies on the same day on which he was born. The *Idylls* also begin and end with a darkness which is prelude to the light: in *The Coming of Arthur,* Arthur is born on the night of the new year and comes as the sun to lighten the dark world. *The Passing of Arthur* ends with "the new sun . . . bringing the new year" (469).

Both the cyclical and circular structures of the *Idylls* are reinforced and clarified by the repetition in the first and last books of a single line, which indicates in one sense at least that we have come full circle and end where we began. In *The Coming of Arthur,* Arthur refuses to pay tribute to Rome and maintains that " 'The old order changeth, yielding place to new' " (508). His refusal marks the rejection of both the paganism which Rome traditionally represented and the spiritually enervated Christianity which it presently represents. It is important to see that the order which changes is not only social but spiritual in order to understand clearly Arthur's repetition of the line in *The Passing of Arthur.* We have come full circle and completed a cycle when a dying Arthur says, " 'The old order changeth, yielding place to new, / And God fulfils himself in many ways, / Lest one good custom should corrupt the world' " (408–10). As a degenerate Rome must give way to the spiritually advanced kingdom of Arthur, so must the degenerate Arthurian kingdom give way to another in spiritual advance of it, working out through national history the universal history of mankind. The cycle which is suggested by the repetition of the line is a cycle which is continually repeated as mankind moves toward its providential end.

The cyclical metaphors which serve Tennyson in the *Idylls* as structural devices are of course more than a means of providing the poem with a structure. They also contribute to the poem's unity as they are reflections of the poem's historicism. In other words, the cyclical metaphors are not added by Tennyson to the poem; they grow out of the poem's subject matter. They are organic and, because they are organic and all related to one another, they not only structure the poem but unify it.

The *Idylls* has also been thought to be unified through the central character of Arthur and through the theme of "Soul against Sense." Hallam Tennyson defends the poem's unity in this way: "To sum up: if Epic unity is looked for in the 'Idylls,' we find it not in the wrath of an Achilles, nor in the wanderings of an Ulysses, but in the unending war of humanity in all ages, —the world-wide war of Sense and Soul, typified in individuals, with the subtle interaction of character upon character, the central dominant figure being the pure, generous, tender, brave, human-hearted Arthur—so that the links (with here and there symbolic accessories) which bind the 'Idylls' into an artistic whole, are perhaps somewhat intricate." [25] Intricate indeed, one might add, as it seems to me that the central character of Arthur and the thematic description of Sense at war with Soul have done more to confuse the issue than to clarify it.

To begin with, because the earliest idyll, *Morte d'Arthur,* was written within a few weeks of Arthur Hallam's death and appears in manuscript with the earliest verses of *In Memoriam,* it is not surprising that one can find autobiographical overtones in it. It is perhaps likely that Tennyson cast himself in the role of Bedivere and Hallam in the role of the king. The *Morte d'Arthur* may then be read as an autobiographical reconciliation to death and a dedication to poetry, perhaps to *In Memoriam,* as Bedivere is counseled by the king to "let thy voice / Rise like a fountain for me night and day" (*The Passing of Arthur,* 416–17). More important, however, than hypothetical autobiographical significance in the poem is the relation between the Arthur of *In Memoriam* and the Arthur of the *Idylls* which their juxtaposition in the Commonplace Book seems to suggest. I submit that in *In Memoriam* Tennyson attempted to idealize the real man, while in the *Idylls* he attempted to realize the ideal man. Both Arthurs therefore meet. [26] And though the first poem is concerned with the individual and the second with society, both deal with the spirit in a world of matter.

25. *Memoir,* p. 526.
26. Both Arthurs are, of course, given Christlike qualities.

It seems to me that Tennyson is more successful at idealizing the real Arthur of *In Memoriam* than he is in realizing the ideal Arthur of the *Idylls*. The poet's problem is that he apparently wished to make King Arthur a real character at the same time that he expected him to carry the allegorical burden of representing the soul. That he did not succeed to his own satisfaction is perhaps indicated by his attempt to clarify this point in his final addition to the *Epilogue to the Queen* (1891) of this line to describe Arthur—"ideal manhood closed in real man" (38).[27] If Arthur represents Soul, then it is perhaps Lancelot who ought to be the central character of the poem, as it is most clearly he who is torn between his love for Arthur, or soul, and his love for Guinevere, or sense. The roles of Arthur and Guinevere would then be primarily "allegorical," as there would be no necessity for them to be *real* characters any more than there is for a Billy Budd or a Claggart to be *real*. And yet it is clear that it is Arthur, not Lancelot, who is the central figure of the poem. His inability to play both roles as real character and allegorical figure has caused general confusion.

This confusion is compounded by the thematic description of soul at war with sense. It is possible for Arthur to play his allegorical role of "soul" when he comes to the chaotic world of the kingdoms, clearly a world of unbridled sense, to unify them. He does so as an infusion of soul or spirit to drive out the beast and lighten the dark world. In another context, Arthur's "allegorical" role is impossible. If Arthur represents "soul" and Guinevere represents "sense" or flesh, if you will, then the poem should take the form of Arthur's war against Guinevere, which, of course, it cannot.

There is a fundamental confusion, which Tennyson seems to have shared, in describing the relation between soul and sense as a war. On the one hand, it is true that soul should war lest sense conquer. Man becomes less than man, becomes beast, when soul is conquered by sense, and this is certainly undesirable. But on the other hand, soul cannot annihilate sense or man is not man either. Man is a combination of soul and sense, or flesh and spirit, and to be deficient in either is to lack the *manness* common to men; it is to be more than human or less than human. Arthur,

27. See *Memoir*, p. 526.

for example, is deficient in flesh, and it is for this reason perhaps that critics have been unhappy with his character, which seems to lack the human reality of a Lancelot or a Guinevere.

Tennyson's own ambivalence both about the theme of the *Idylls* and about the role of Arthur is quite evident. Though it is perhaps an overstatement to say that "the 'blameless King' . . . is paradoxically to blame for the destruction of his own kingdom," [28] it is true that Arthur is not really blameless. The first four lines of the *Idylls* are these:

> Leodogran, the King of Cameliard,
> Had one fair daughter, and none other child;
> And she was fairest of all flesh on earth,
> Guinevere, and in her his one delight.

Guinevere is flesh, however fair. And Arthur later says,

> '. . . for saving I be joined
> To her that is the fairest under heaven,
> I seem as nothing in the mighty world,
> And cannot will my will, nor work my work
> Wholly, nor make myself in mine own realm
> Victor and lord. But were I joined with her,
> Then might we live together as one life,
> And reigning with one will in everything
> Have power on this dark land to lighten it,
> And power on this dead world to make it live.'
>
> (84–93)

It is clear that the soul or spirit which Arthur represents is powerless without joining flesh. [29] Arthur must not, nor does he wish to, conquer Guinevere; soul is not at war with sense. On the contrary, he must join with her to become one. The welding of soul and sense, or flesh and spirit, alone can produce harmony, not the war of one against the other. It is Arthur's inability to join

---

28. Solomon, "Tennyson's Paradoxical King," p. 259.

29. See the novice's tale in *Guinevere* (296–99): "and could he [Arthur] find / A woman in her womanhood as great / As he was in his manhood, then, he sang, / The twain together well might change the world." It seems clear that Arthur cannot work his work independently; he must as soul join with flesh just as he must as man join with woman.

with flesh which is at once his aesthetic failure in the poem and his moral failure in the kingdom. Though he does not war with Guinevere, neither does he join with her, except nominally through the ceremony of marriage,[30] and he thereby contributes to the destruction of the kingdom.

One cannot discount completely Guinevere's remarks to Lancelot in *Lancelot and Elaine:*

> 'Arthur, my lord, Arthur, the faultless King,
> That passionate perfection, my good lord—
> But who can gaze upon the Sun in heaven?
> He never spake word of reproach to me,
> He never had a glimpse of mine untruth,
> He cares not for me: only here today
> There gleamed a vague suspicion in his eyes:
> Some meddling rogue has tampered with him—else
> Rapt in this fancy of his Table Round,
> And swearing men to vows impossible,
> To make them like himself: but, friend, to me
> He is all fault who hath no fault at all:
> For who loves me must have a touch of earth;
> The low sun makes the colour. . . ." (121–34)

There is truth in what she says. Admittedly Guinevere as flesh is perhaps too little concerned with spirit, but her infidelity has not necessarily affected her judgment. She has the ability to see and value virtue, if not to be virtuous: she says to Lancelot, " 'I for you / This many a year have done despite and wrong / To one whom ever in my heart of hearts / I did acknowledge nobler' " (*Lancelot and Elaine*, 1201–4). She is able quite justly to recognize at once Arthur's nobility and his want of "a touch of earth."

Of course Guinevere is guilty, but to admit her guilt is not to

---

30. Cf. Johnson, "The Theme of Marriage in Tennyson," p. 8: "The social failure of Arthur is a failure of marriage, a failure that implies the disintegration of his ideal world. It is also, from another point of view, a failure of the Manichean heresy that would separate the spirit from the flesh; for Tennyson's hero is a god who fails to become man." Guinevere's remark (*Guinevere*, 402–4) about her response on first seeing Arthur seems to reflect Arthur's failure to become man: she "thought him cold, / High, self-contained, and passionless, not like him, / 'Not like my Lancelot.' "

exonerate Arthur. In *Balin and Balan,* as we saw in Chapter 4, Lancelot recounts to the Queen a dream:

> '. . . Last night methought I saw
> That maiden Saint who stands with lily in hand
> In yonder shrine. All round her prest the dark,
> And all the light upon her silver face
> Flowed from the spiritual lily that she held.
> Lo! these her emblems drew mine eyes—away:
> For see, how perfect-pure! As light a flush
> As hardly tints the blossom of the quince
> Would mar their charm of stainless maidenhood.'
>   (255–63)

The Queen answers, " 'Sweeter to me' she said 'this garden rose / Deep-hued and many-folded!' " (264–65). More is meant here than that Guinevere chooses passion over innocence. In the first place, Lancelot associates the lily not with innocence or purity, but with spirit; it is a "spiritual lily." The rose is in contradistinction to it. The rose associated with Guinevere is regularly associated with flesh.[31] In rejecting the lily in favor of the rose, Guinevere shows herself to be one-sided. She is not like Maud "Queen lily and rose in one," as she would be if she were the harmonious combination of flesh and spirit that she should be. She rejects the spiritual lily as she rejected the spiritual Arthur or as Lancelot rejects the spiritual Elaine, but unlike Lancelot's guilt, the fault is not hers alone. As she has rejected the spirit, Arthur has rejected or ignored the flesh. For all Vivien's unreliability, there is some truth in what she says of Arthur:

> 'Man! is he man at all, who knows and winks?
> Sees what his fair bride is and does, and winks?
> By which the good King means to blind himself,
> And blinds himself and all the Table Round
> To all the foulness that they work. Myself
> Could call him (were it not for womanhood)

---

31. Ettare, for example, in *Pelleas and Ettare* is both flesh and rose: "her bloom / [is] a rosy dawn kindled in stainless heavens" as "The beauty of her flesh abashed the boy" (67–68, 74). Pelleas finds Ettare and Gawain in a pavilion pitched in a "garden, all / Of roses white and red" (412–13); and in the song about the rose (391–400) the rose is associated with both Ettare and Guinevere.

The pretty, popular name such manhood earns,
Could call him the main cause of all their crime;
Yea, were he not crowned King, coward, and fool.'
                              (*Merlin and Vivien,* 779–87)

Arthur, of course, does not "wink" at Guinevere's transgressions, but he has not joined with her; he and Guinevere do not apparently "live together as one life." If the queen's guilty passion for Lancelot contributes to the destruction of the kingdom, as most critics believe, then Arthur's inadequacy becomes a condition, if not a cause, of that destruction, and his moral responsibility is palpable though his may have been a sin of omission rather than a sin of commission.

The confusion, then, which surrounds the *Idylls,* the confusion about the allegorical roles filled by the characters in the war of soul against sense, seems to be a confusion which Tennyson himself shared. If these things are not clear in the poem, it is because Tennyson is not clear. If Arthur and Guinevere do not bend satisfactorily to their allegorical roles, it is perhaps because Tennyson looks upon them ambivalently.

If the *Idylls of the King* is looked at from another perspective, a perspective wherein the theme is not assumed to be soul at war with sense and Arthur and Guinevere are seen only as members of the cast rather than principal actors, the poem seems less confused. There is a theme, I believe, which runs clearly and consistently throughout the poem and which is one of the poem's major concerns.

6. *Idylls of the King:* The Poem

IT WILL be remembered that after the earliest book, *Morte d'Arthur* of 1833, Tennyson abandoned the Arthurian world and turned his attention to *The Princess* (published in 1847), a poem concerned with "a social question—the position of women in life."[1] When Tennyson returned to the romance, he produced *Enid, Vivien, Elaine,* and *Guinevere,* significantly naming after women the first four idylls to appear as *Idylls.* Apparently the woman question, with which he had dealt in *The Princess,* was still a very real one for him—and so it would seem when the *Idylls* is taken as a whole.

Though it has been said that "the theme of marital disharmony, as surely every critic has pointed out, is central to the *Idylls,*"[2] it is not marital disharmony in any limited sense which is central, as after all few of the characters are married. It is rather the relation between men and women, or more specifically the role women play in individual redemption or destruction and in social integration or dissolution, which is central to the poem. As one of a whole series of such relationships, the relationship between Arthur and Guinevere is an example not merely of the failure of soul to wed with sense, but of the failure of man to join with woman, his complement. Wendell Stacy Johnson is surely right in his suggestion that "The social failure of Arthur is a failure of marriage, a failure that implies the disintegration of his ideal world."[3] If we take marriage in its largest sense to

1. Killham, *Tennyson and "The Princess,"* p. 1. Some lines from a manuscript version of *The Princess* became part of the early *Enid;* see Ricks, *Poems,* p. 1535n.
2. Poston, III, "The Argument of the Geraint-Enid Books in *Idylls of the King,*" p. 269.
3. "The Theme of Marriage in Tennyson," p. 8.

mean the complementary relationship between man and woman, we can see in the *Idylls* how its neglect or perversion does indeed lead to disintegration. Because women have great powers for good and evil, it is as destructive to neglect the influence of a good woman as it is to submit to the influence of a bad one.

A thematic consideration of the position of women in the *Idylls* is of course only one of many options open to a critic. I have chosen it because it seems to me that the woman question is more or less central to all the books of "The Round Table" and because it is perhaps the most significant and revolutionary question of the nineteenth century. Certainly Tennyson was "modern" in addressing himself to the woman question; whether he was modern in his understanding of it must await the examination of the books of "The Round Table."

*

In the first of the books of "The Round Table," *Gareth and Lynette,* we are introduced to the problems of the transitional periods from childhood to youth and from youth to manhood. The time is appropriately spring and Gareth is the young and untried knight and Lynette the young and innocent maiden. And like the young nation which is emerging from its infancy and testing the virtues by which it may succeed, Gareth emancipates himself from his mother, Bellicent, and goes to the court of Arthur to undergo the tests which certify him a man. Arthur enumerates the virtues to which he must adhere—hardihood, gentleness, faithfulness in love, and obedience to the king (541–44)—and Gareth had previously determined to "follow the Christ, the King, / Live pure, speak true, right wrong, follow the King" (116–17). His hardiness and his righting of wrong are tested in his knightly battles; his obedience is tested by his mother, by the seneschal, Sir Kay, and by Arthur; but his gentleness, his purity, and his faithfulness are all tested by Lynette.

Lynette is, however, more than simply a test, though she is that. Clearly her role is twofold: she is at once a test of Gareth's courtesy, as in Malory, and she is a source of encouragement in his tests of knightly valor. Gareth makes both roles apparent when he tells her

'. . . . You said your say;
Mine answer was my deed. Good sooth! I hold
He scarce is knight, yea but half-man, nor meet
To fight for gentle damsel, he, who lets
His heart be stirred with any foolish heat
At any gentle damsel's waywardness.
Shamed? care not! thy foul sayings fought for me:
And seeing now thy words are fair, methinks
There rides no knight, not Lancelot, his great self,
Hath force to quell me.' (1145–54)

When Lynette derides him, her derision sends the "strength of anger" (926) through his arms; when she speaks him fair, he feels himself unconquerable. In either case she encourages the valor which allows him to overcome his knightly opponents in his allegorical journey through life. And her derision as clearly tests Gareth's courtesy and gentleness as his battles test his valor. She is, like Ettare, a trial of faith for the untried knight. But her influence is obviously good because she contributes to Gareth's maturation, whereas Ettare contributes to Pelleas' destruction.

Gareth's quest and Lynette's role in it are more than personal; they are socially significant. The values which are tested in the person of Gareth are values fundamental to Arthur's kingdom. In a sense, as the young knight prospers in the righting of wrongs through the exercise of valor, courtesy, and gentleness, so through their exercise can the young nation prosper. But the success of the individual or the nation seems to be in some way proportional to the beneficent or maleficent influence of women. If the quarrelsome Lynette is not the perfect or near-perfect woman, her influence is nevertheless beneficial. She is young and is learning her role, as Gareth is learning his, for youth is the age of tutelage. If Lynette lacks the maturity and grace of an Enid or an Elaine, neither is she an Ettare.

In the two Geraint and Enid books which follow, a different age, no longer youth; a different relationship, between man and wife; and different types of characters are explored. Where Gareth was the center of the previous idyll, Enid is the center of these two books, which were originally published, as I have said, together under the title *Enid*. And, of course, Enid, as a model of modesty, just obedience, patience, and fidelity, contrasts sharply to the volatile, strong-willed, impetuous Lynette. Moreover, Enid's role in the idylls in which she appears is not only more central than Lynette's, but it is also considerably more complex, as she is the primary force in the spiritual regeneration and social integration of two men—Edyrn and Geraint.

Edyrn, the nephew of Yniol and cousin of Enid, in pride and anger at Enid's refusal of him, has stolen his uncle's earldom [4] and lives a life which he describes in retrospect as "wellnigh mad" (*G and E*, 835). Enid, Edyrn tells us, is the cause, though blameless, of his sin: "Yourself were first the blameless cause to make / My nature's prideful sparkle in the blood / Break into furious flame" (*G and E*, 825–27). But she is also, as Tennyson makes clear, his means to contrition and subsequent redemption, for though Geraint vows on four separate occasions to break Edyrn's pride, it is really Enid who does so.[5] At the mock tournament [6] of the sparrow-hawk, Geraint overthrows Edyrn, who admits, " 'My pride is broken: men have seen my fall' " (*M of G*, 578), but later tells Geraint, " 'For I have never yet been overthrown, / And thou hast overthrown me, and my pride / Is broken down, for Enid sees my fall!' " (*M of G*, 588–90). From this point of contrition, Edyrn goes through penance to salvation, as he himself suggests: " 'There was I broken down; there was I saved' " (*G and E*, 850).[7] Geraint, after overthrowing Edyrn in the tournament, sends him to court to crave pardon of the Queen, who requires as "penance" (*G and E*, 853) only that he rest awhile at court. There he learns the virtues of the Round Table and turns, we are told, from hate to love and from an anti-social life to one of social significance:

4. Tennyson differs here from the *Mabinogion*. See Harold Littledale, *Essays on Lord Tennyson's "Idylls of the King"* (London, 1893), pp. 120–21; also Ricks, *Poems*, pp. 1539–40nn.

5. I differ here from Buckley (*Tennyson*, p. 179), who refers to Edyrn as "the villain whose reform Geraint himself has effected."

6. Like Gareth's small lie, which foreshadows the lies which destroy the kingdom, Edyrn's tournament, where he does his paramour "mock-honour as the fairest fair" (*G and E*, 832), seems to foreshadow the mockery of the Last Tournament, where Tristram is the purest knight and Isolt the purest maid.

7. Edyrn may mean that his life was spared, but Arthur suggests his spiritual salvation when he echoes the parable of the lost sheep in speaking of Edyrn's reformation. See *G and E*, 910–18.

And being young, he changed and came to loathe
His crime of traitor, slowly drew himself
Bright from his old dark life, and fell at last
In the great battle fighting for the King.
(*M of G,* 593–96)

Edyrn quite clearly owes both his spiritual redemption and his
social integration in considerable part to women, to the Queen
and to Enid.

Enid's role in the redemption and integration of Geraint is
similar to the one she plays with respect to Edyrn, though here is
involved the love of a good woman for her husband. Geraint,
though his sin is different from that of Edyrn, is no less seriously
sinful and in need of redemption. Geraint's uxoriousness, the sin
traditionally attributed to Adam, has made him not only effeminate but socially useless; he has become

Forgetful of his promise to the King,
Forgetful of the falcon and the hunt,
Forgetful of the tilt and tournament,
Forgetful of his glory and his name,
Forgetful of his princedom and its cares.
(*M of G,* 50–54)

Geraint's sin of uxoriousness is, like Adam's, compounded by
distrust, a lack of faith, ingratitude, disobedience, infidelity, discourtesy. In subordinating all things to his love for Enid, Geraint
has failed to place woman in her proper sphere. Enid does not
require his submission nor can she submit herself entirely to
obedience to him. What marriage and a useful life require is a
harmonious and complementary relationship between man and
woman. As the disharmony and inversion of their relationship is
suggested by Enid's riding before Geraint through the wilderness,
so is the proper relationship between them rendered dramatically
after their reconciliation: she takes his hand and sets her foot on
his to mount behind him on his horse; he kisses her and she en-
circles him with her arms; and we are told, she "Put hand to hand
beneath her husband's heart, / And felt him hers again" (*G and
E,* 749–67).

Geraint's salvation is not so clearly suggested as Edyrn's. But as with Edyrn, that period of his sinful life is described as "madness"[8] (a madness which is perhaps as in *Maud* a symbolic death[9]) and he is restored by the love of a good woman. More palpable is Geraint's social regeneration. Like Maud, Enid quite obviously wishes to encourage the social responsibility of warring for the good. Distraught by the charges of effeminacy and uxoriousness made against Geraint, she says,

> 'And yet I hate that he should linger here;
> I cannot love my lord and not his name.
> Far liefer had I gird his harness on him,
> And ride with him to battle and stand by,
> And watch his mightful hand striking great blows
> At caitiffs and at wrongers of the world.'
>
> (*M of G,* 91–96)

Such a desire on the part of Enid is little different from Maud's "hope for the world in the coming wars." In both poems, it seems to me, the poet is dealing not only with the redemption of the individual, but also with the role which women play in encouraging social responsibility simply by being good women. Lawrence Poston III is right when he says that "Geraint and Edyrn are redeemed, but the kingdom is merely reformed. . . . A lasting social reform becomes increasingly unlikely; redemption remains personal."[10] It is no less true, however, that regardless of the possibility of a permanent social reformation, the redeemed man lives a life of social service fighting against the powers of wickedness. In so doing he serves God's purpose even if he cannot restore paradise to earth. As the redeemed hero of *Maud* "embraced the purpose of God, and the doom assigned," which was to go off to war, so do the redeemed Edyrn and Geraint meet their deaths in like endeavors: as we saw, Edyrn "fell at last / In the great battle fighting for the King" and Geraint, we are told,

---

8. In some rather confusing lines toward the end of *Geraint and Enid* (811–12) Geraint hesitates to face Arthur, "Fearing the mild face of the blameless King, / And after madness acted question asked."

9. Cf. Poston, "The Argument of the Geraint-Enid books," p. 274: "Geraint passes from grace through a form of spiritual madness to redemption."

10. Ibid., p. 275.

> . . . crowned
> A happy life with a fair death, and fell
> Against the heathen of the Northern Sea
> In battle, fighting for the blameless King.
> (*G and E,* 966–69)

Women are important, then, for both the spiritual and social
direction which they afford. They are also important as the means
of bringing both the individual and the society to fruition. The
last we hear of Enid is that she has become

> . . . Enid, whom her ladies loved to call
> Enid the Fair, a grateful people named
> Enid the Good; and in their halls arose
> The cry of children, Enids and Geraints
> Of times to be. . . .   (*G and E,* 961–65)

Here in the third book of "The Round Table" is the last union of
the *Idylls* which comes to fruition. By the time one gets to the end
of *Lancelot and Elaine,* as we shall see, all hope for generation in
the kingdom has come to an end.

The next idyll, *Balin and Balan,* is connected to the Geraint-
Enid books in several ways. Both stories deal with madness of a
sort, though it is obviously more violent in Balin than in Geraint
or Edyrn.[11] Both deal with the role of women in the reformation
of an individual from a life of violence.[12] In both the parable of
the lost sheep is evoked,[13] but where the lost sheep is found in
Geraint and Enid, he remains lost in *Balin and Balan* because the
salutary influence of the good woman is withdrawn and the
pernicious influence of the bad woman is introduced. Not only,
in other words, does Balin lose the wholesome influence of Guinevere; he is subjected to the evil influence of Vivien, and the result
is destruction.

The tale of the two brothers who come together from one
womb and go together to one grave is a kind of Tennysonian

11. Both Geraint's and Balin's madness are alike triggered by their suspicion of
the Queen's infidelity.

12. The violence from which Balin suffers is like that in Edyrn before his pride
is broken. Arthur describes that portion of Edyrn's life as "a life of violence" in
Geraint and Enid, 912.

13. Cf. *Geraint and Enid,* 910–18, and *Balin and Balan,* 78.

study of the split mind. Balin, who represents the raw, passionate, willful side of man's nature, must be controlled by Balan, who represents the reasonable, responsible, and dutiful side. When these two aspects of man's personality work together, they can produce the socially active and responsible individual. When they are in conflict, as they are at the end of the idyll, they produce destruction. Balan is not, however, the only one with the capacity to control Balin's violence. When his violence is severed from the control of his brother, who alone has had power over it, Balin seeks a new means of control, and he finds it by emulating Lancelot, who owes his growth, his name, his strength, his gentleness (178–80) to his worship of the Queen. Guinevere, then, can exert the influence which will allow Balin to control his violence, as twice she does, first when he is tempted to strike the thrall who caused his banishment and second when he is tempted to hurl the goblet at Garlon.[14] But the influence of the "fairest, best and purest" (345), which had brought Lancelot "might, / Name, manhood, and a grace" (371–72) loses its efficacy as the Queen's name becomes tainted, for the vague rumor of the Queen's infidelity, which drove Geraint to madness, becomes in *Balin and Balan* more palpable, though not proven. Loosed from the control of the good woman, Balin falls prey to the control of an evil one. And an idyll which begins with the reassertion of the principle enunciated in *The Coming of Arthur*—"Man's word is God in man"—ends with the introduction of Vivien, who lies with ease, and the loss of Balin, who, Arthur tells us, "hast ever spoken truth" (70).

Balin and Balan deals not only with the place of women in individual redemption or destruction; it deals as well with woman's social role. In the idyll two antithetical but equally degenerate societies, which have rejected the spiritual advance of Arthur's kingdom, are introduced. There is first the spiritually stagnant court of Pellam, which with its emphasis on celibacy, asceticism, idolatrous worship of saints, phony relics, and golden altars, even perhaps a kind of apostolic succession in Pellam's attempt to trace his descent from Joseph of Arimathea, is evocative of the spiritually decadent Rome from which Arthur has freed himself. There is also introduced the spiritually retrogres-

14. See 214–20, 363–65.

sive kingdom of King Mark, represented by Vivien. Mark's is a beastly and sensual society associated in Vivien's song about sun-worship (434–49) with druidical paganism. Equally degenerate as the two societies are, they are at the same time antithetical, as they represent two extremes.

This antithetical nature is suggested first by Vivien, whose song specifically rejects the asceticism which we associate in the idyll with Pellam's court:

> 'Old priest, who mumble worship in your quire—
> Old monk and nun, ye scorn the world's desire,
> Yet in your frosty cells ye feel the fire!
> The fire of Heaven is not the flame of Hell.'   (438–41)

And just as specifically is the society represented by Vivien rejected by Pellam, who drives her from his gates (598–602). Both societies, antithetical as they are, share a common fatal defect—the role of women in either is neglected or perverted. Pellam, when he takes "as in rival heat, to holy things" (97), pushes "aside his faithful wife, nor lets / Or dame or damsel enter at his gates" (103–4). In foolishly attempting to pursue the spirit by rejecting the flesh, Pellam has ironically banished women, the means to spiritual enlightenment. Vivien, on the other hand, represents the perversion rather than the neglect of women in society. Mark's kingdom is a society given over to sensuality, where women are turned into harlots. Mark's is a society fatally flawed by its neglect of the spirit in pursuit of the flesh.[15] Pellam's in contrast is equally flawed because it falsely pursues the spirit by excluding the flesh.

As the Geraint-Enid books had demonstrated that men subject to the influence of good women could be spiritually redeemed and brought to social use, so does *Balin and Balan* demonstrate the contrary—that men not subject to the influence of gentle women or men subject to the influence of perverse women are

---

15. The sensuality of Mark's kingdom is reflected in part in the besotted squire who attends Vivien: he is the living dog which, in a paraphrase of Ecclesiastes 9:4, she prefers to the dead lion (573–74). The squire's love for Vivien has, of course, turned him into a beast. He is both a dog and "Sir Chick," and his willingness to lie for her denies the spirit, for as Arthur repeatedly says in the poem "Man's word is God in man."

alike liable to social or moral irresponsibility. If that is at least in part the theme of *Balin and Balan,* it is no less the theme of the following idyll.

Vivien appears again in the next idyll, *Merlin and Vivien,* where her power is seen as more terrible because it is exercised not on the boy squire or the half-mad Balin, but on the aged and intellectual Merlin. When the sage succumbs to the lamia-like Vivien, she, who in *Balin and Balan* had been a Circe or an Acrasia, has become a Delilah or an Eve. Merlin himself suggests Vivien's role when he associates her curiosity with that of Eve: "Too much I trusted when I told you that, / And stirred this vice in you which ruined man / Through woman the first hour" (359–61). Though the tale of Merlin's destruction at the hands of Vivien may illustrate, as E. D. H. Johnson suggests, "Tennyson's distrust of reason when it is not supported by some form of transcendental faith," [16] it seems to me that Merlin (though of course he is not married to Vivien) illustrates the sin of an excessive uxoriousness. Somewhat like Geraint, but more like Adam, Merlin has allowed Vivien a dominance which violates the proper complementary relationship between men and women. Indeed, Merlin is more guilty than Adam: if Eve, who deserved Adam's love, does not deserve his subordination, how much less is Vivien, who does not deserve Merlin's love, entitled to dominance? Enid knew the dangers of an excessive uxoriousness and was the agent of her husband's spiritual and social redemption; Vivien is, of course, her antithesis.

Jerome Buckley is surely right in his conclusion that "Merlin's yielding to the seductive wiles of Vivien is . . . the grossest example of the abject surrender of the intellect to the flesh"; [17] but it would be a mistake, I think, for one to assume that Vivien represents only flesh. She represents as well the hatred which destroys as opposed to the love which saves, as she indicates by her inversion of the scriptural text about love which she paraphrases: "As Love, if Love be perfect, casts out fear, / So Hate, if Hate be perfect, casts out fear" (40–41). [18] Born of death rather

16. *The Alien Vision,* p. 50.

17. *Tennyson,* pp. 181–82.

18. Vivien's incapacity for love is suggested in her comment on the dream of Lancelot and Guinevere, who dream of each other—"The mortal dream that never

than life (44), Vivien is not only the instrument for Merlin's destruction, but she is the vehicle for the lie, which marks so strikingly the decline of the kingdom.

Merlin's choice of Vivien, then, is more complex than the simple choice of flesh. If he is not clearly guilty of all the sins attributed to Adam by Milton,[19] he is at least guilty of a selfishness which is not only personally destructive, but detrimental to society. In choosing self over the claims of society, Merlin is lost because, unlike the soul in *The Palace of Art,* for example, he is not afforded the time for contrition and subsequent redemption through social service. Merlin's social significance and the importance of his loss to society should not be forgotten just because he is old: he is "the most famous man of all those times" (164); he is

> Merlin, who knew the range of all their arts,
> Had built the King his havens, ships, and halls,
> Was also Bard, and knew the starry heavens;
> The people called him Wizard. . . .   (165–68)

Being most famous, Merlin has the greatest opportunity for use; as he says himself,

> '. . . but Fame with men,
> Being but ampler means to serve mankind,
> Should have small rest or pleasure in herself,
> But work as vassal to the larger love,
> That dwarfs the petty love of one to one.
> Use gave me Fame at first, and Fame again
> Increasing gave me use. . . .'   (486–92)

Merlin's choice of Vivien, then, is not only self-destructive, but in his choice he forfeits that use which he so highly prizes and contributes to the doom which he foresees—the destruction of the kingdom. As Milton says of Adam—"Against his better knowledge, not deceiv'd, / But fondly overcome with Female charm"

---

yet was mine" (115). Littledale understands Vivien's remark similarly (p. 177). The scriptural text is I John 4:18, "There is no fear in love; but perfect love casteth out fear: because fear hath torment. He that feareth is not made perfect in love."

19. See Merritt Hughes' edition of *Paradise Lost* (New York, 1962), p. 235*n.*

—so might one say of Merlin. The responsibility for his sin is clearly his, though the perverse woman contributes to his destruction. At any rate, with the loss of Merlin the kingdom has taken another step in a decline which by the end of the next idyll is irreversible.

Tennyson seems to have maintained a sort of contrapuntal structure in the introduction of women into the early idylls.[20] We are first introduced to the rather petulant Lynette, then the perfect Enid; she is followed by a vicious Vivien, who is in turn followed by the spiritual Elaine, the "lily maid of Astolat." Tennyson had dealt with the maid who lived in fantasy and died for the love of Lancelot as early as 1832 in *The Lady of Shalott,* but there are few similarities between that poem and the sixth book of "The Round Table." *Lancelot and Elaine* owes much to Malory, but some Tennysonian changes and additions provide a continuity with the other books of the *Idylls.*

In the first place, Malory refers to the "Fayre Maydyn off Astolot" or "Elayne le Blanke"; it is Tennyson who refers to her as the "lily maid" (some twelve times) and adds to the description of her death the lily in her hand. Long ago Harold Littledale referred to "the lily, needless emblem of purity, in Elaine's hand,"[21] but it seems to me that Tennyson is too insistent with the image and too careful a poet continually to associate the lily with Elaine if it is no more than a needless emblem of purity. If one remembers Lancelot's dream of the spiritual lily and Guinevere's identification with the rose in *Balin and Balan* (255–64), it becomes apparent that the dream and Guinevere's comment foreshadow the later reality of Lancelot's choice between the lily and the rose. When he chooses Guinevere rather than Elaine, he has rather clearly chosen the rose rather than the lily, the flesh over the spirit.[22] I do not mean to suggest that Elaine is a mere

20. He apparently had such a structure in mind when he originally entitled the earliest *Idylls* published *The True and the False.* See Sir Charles Tennyson, *Tennyson,* p. 316.

21. *Essays on Lord Tennyson's "Idylls of the King,"* p. 204.

22. I am in disagreement here with Buckley, who feels that Elaine "betrays her own purity." He says, "Elaine is appropriately 'the lily maid of Astolat,' and in death she holds the white flower against her white robe; but the passion which destroys her is clearly represented by a scarlet sleeve that Lancelot carries to the tourney as her token" (*Tennyson,* pp. 182–83). Because Tennyson borrows the

allegorical representation of spirit. She functions also as a kind of pre-lapsarian Eve, a woman naturally good, who, somewhat after the manner of Eve, stands "Rapt on [Lancelot's] face as if it were a God's" (354).[23] It is even suggested in the poem that she is comparable only to pre-lapsarian Eve:

> Meeker than any child to a rough nurse,
> Milder than any mother to a sick child,
> And never woman yet, since man's first fall,
> Did kindlier unto man, but her deep love
> Upbore her. . . .   (852–56)

Lancelot, on the other hand, is a kind of post-lapsarian Adam; he is "a living soul" (252), perhaps as Adam is the "living soul" distinguished from the "quickening spirit." I mean to make no elaborate analogy here, only to suggest that Lancelot is, like Adam, the natural man in need of redemption. Already disobedient, he cannot choose obedience, the path to salvation for pre-lapsarian man, but must be redeemed. In other words, what Lancelot already *is* determines the choices open to him.

Lancelot's choice of Guinevere rather than Elaine is not naïvely made. He admits that Elaine "loved me with a love beyond all love / In women, whomsoever I have known" (1284–85) and he clearly suspects the impermanence of Guinevere's love for him.[24] His choice of Guinevere, however, is inevitable, not because man is denied free will, but because the moral choices open to any man are determined by those which he has already made. An old Lancelot, who has already chosen Guinevere before he meets Elaine, is not really free to choose the spiritual purity which Elaine represents any more than the sinful man can choose to be

---

red sleeve from Malory, perhaps less importance should be attached to it than to the lily, which Tennyson introduces. Tennyson further eliminates from his borrowing Malory's description of Elaine as "so hot in love" and her explicit offer to be Lancelot's paramour. I do not see that the love which Elaine dies for is equated by Tennyson with passion, as it clearly is in Malory. Cf. Malory, Book XVIII, with *Lancelot and Elaine,* 930–58.

23. Cf. *Paradise Lost,* Book IV, 296–99, 636–38.
24. He says of Guinevere's love,
> Queen, if I grant the jealousy as of love,
> May not your crescent fear for name and fame
> Speak, as it waxes, of a love that wanes?   (1388–90)

sinless. And to choose Elaine would, of course, necessitate a further violation of the virtues of the Round Table. Tennyson makes Lancelot's dilemma clear:

> And peradventure had he seen her first
> She might have made this and that other world
> Another world for the sick man; but now
> The shackles of an old love straitened him,
> His honour rooted in dishonour stood,
> And faith unfaithful kept him falsely true.   (867–72)

The choice of Elaine would involve him in further dishonor, infidelity, and falsity.

Arthur also seems to recognize both the impossibility of Lancelot's choice of Elaine and the potential good which is thereby forfeited. He says,

> '. . . but now I would to God,
> Seeing the homeless trouble in thine eyes,
> Thou couldst have loved this maiden, shaped, it seems,
> By God for thee alone, and from her face,
> If one may judge the living by the dead,
> Delicately pure and marvellously fair,
> Who might have brought thee, now a lonely man
> Wifeless and heirless, noble issue, sons
> Born to the glory of thy name and fame,
> My knight, the great Sir Lancelot of the Lake.'   (1353–62)

But the loss of Elaine is more than a personal loss to Lancelot. Lancelot's personal salvation remains possible and we are told "he should die a holy man" (1418), but, because Elaine represents spirit, her rejection and death dramatically render the death of spirit in the kingdom. Personal redemption is possible, but the loss of spirit in the kingdom makes impossible the retardation of social disintegration.

Elaine's death is really the symbolic culmination of a process of disintegration which is manifested in *Lancelot and Elaine* in many ways. First, for the first time in the *Idylls* the sinful relationship between Lancelot and Guinevere is no longer rumor; it is beyond doubt. Second, because Lancelot is Arthur's greatest knight, whom other knights emulate, knowledge of his taint has more serious social consequences than would that of a lesser knight, and it is important that the taint is now within the kingdom, not without among the heathen, in the court of Mark or Pellam. Third, if at least part of Arthur's virtue lies in the fact that he "honours his own word, / As if it were his God's" (143–44), the process of dissolution is evident, not only in the introduction of Gawain, who tells the truth only when it suits his purpose, but in the lies of Lancelot and Guinevere and their attitude toward those lies—Lancelot's only remorse for a lie to Arthur apparently being that he "lied in vain" (102). Fourth, the kingdom's social purpose breaks down through disobedience and discourtesy. Gawain, vexed at the quest Arthur has given him, not only fails to perform it, but perverts the role of women by giving the quest to Elaine, "the quest / Assigned to her not worthy of it" (819–20). Fifth, there is the loss of the possibility of fruition in the kingdom through Lancelot's rejection of Elaine, who alone could give him "noble issue, sons / Born to the glory of [his] name and fame." The contrast between the "cry of children, Enids and Geraints / Of times to be" with which *Geraint and Enid* concludes and the sterility with which *Lancelot and Elaine* ends marks the progress toward destruction the kingdom has made. Finally, with the loss of Elaine there is no longer any real possibility of women exercising a salutary influence in the kingdom. With Elaine, spirit in the kingdom dies and there is no longer a chance of retarding the acceleration toward a new barbarity. The kingdom is lost.

In the seventh book of "The Round Table," *The Holy Grail,* those who seek the spirit seek it outside the kingdom and follow wandering fires because the spirit within the kingdom has died. Each knight, with the exception of Bors, selfishly seeks his own salvation, and of course the result is anarchy and destruction. And in this destruction the contribution of women, if not as prominent as in the earlier books, is nevertheless important.

There is, for example, Guinevere, who admits her part in the disintegration of the social order: she says to Lancelot of the knights' vows to pursue the grail, " 'This madness has come on us for our sins' " (357). There are also the merry maidens with whom Gawain dallies rather than pursuing his quest. Of the two women with potential for good, the first is without influence and the second plays only a very minor role. The first, the princess in the castle, chiidhood sweetheart of Percivale, offers him the chance for love and her people offer to make him "as Arthur in [their] land" (605) ; but Percivale rejects her and the opportunity for social service, for when he joins Galahad, he "Cared not for her, nor anything upon earth" (611).[25] The second, the one woman who exerts any positive influence, is the maid who frees Sir Bors from his prison cell.

I have saved the discussion of the holy nun, Percivale's sister, till last, not only because she is the most prominent woman in the idyll, but because her role is most complex as a result of the way in which her character is rendered. Unlike all the other books of "The Round Table," *The Holy Grail* is in the form of a dialogue, and the point of view is largely that of one of the knights rather than that of an omniscient observer. Moreover, the knight who tells the story is the brother of the woman who has such a profound effect on the action and therefore his reliability is at least suspect. One must, in other words, be cautious about accepting what Percivale says. One may grant, for example, that Percivale is pure, as Arthur says he is (3), without accepting Percivale's judgment as right. We have already seen that he has rejected an opportunity to serve mankind, to be an Arthur. It is moreover clear that he has wrongly embarked on a selfish quest which leaves the wrongs of the world to right themselves and brings the destruction of order. And one cannot ignore Arthur's contemptuous allusion to Percivale's choice of the holy life:

> ' "Another hath beheld it [the grail] afar off,
> And leaving human wrongs to right themselves,
> Cares but to pass into the silent life." ' (893–95)

25. Percivale is certainly in contrast to Arthur, who says of his responsibility to rule,

> . . . the King must guard
> That which he rules, and is but as the hind
> To whom a space of land is given to plow.
> Who may not wander from the allotted field
> Before his work be done. . . .   (901–5)

Percivale's error stems from the fact that all men and women are as phantoms to him (564–65). The monk Ambrosius sees more clearly that it is the grail which is the phantom (44).

Percivale's obviously wrong choice of the monastic life for himself makes questionable his objectivity about his sister's similar choice.

There seems to be no question that Percivale's sister is, as Percivale says, a holy maid (70); even Arthur concurs in that judgment (296). But in lines that are rather confusing it appears that she has embraced the holy life because of frustrated love:

> '. . . though never maiden glowed,
> But that was in her earlier maidenhood,
> With such a fervent flame of human love,
> Which being rudely blunted, glanced and shot
> Only to holy things; to prayer and praise
> She gave herself, to fast and alms. . . .'   (72–77)

A blunted human love has apparently caused her (like Pellam, though for different reasons) to take "in rival heat, to holy things." She is holy, but perhaps not wholesomely so. And one cannot seriously question her purity. She is as pure as Galahad, who alone of Arthur's knights is pure enough to see clearly the grail or to ascend into the spiritual city. But the nun manifests her purity in a selfish asceticism of no use to society, whereas Galahad, even while in pursuit of the grail, acts in the world.[26] He tells Percivale,

> ' ". . . And in the strength of this I rode,
> Shattering all evil customs everywhere,
> And past through Pagan realms, and made them mine,
> And clashed with Pagan hordes, and bore them down,
> And broke through all, and in the strength of this
> Come victor. . . ." '   (476–81)

And even Galahad, for whom the quest is most legitimate, is not altogether without censure from Arthur:

> ' "And one hath had the vision face to face,
> And now his chair desires him here in vain,
> However they may crown him otherwise." '   (896–98)

---

26. Galahad's success in pursuit of the grail is the result of his willingness to lose himself to save himself. Nowhere in the idyll is it suggested that the nun loses herself, and of course she does not ascend to the spiritual city as does Galahad.

If the nun's holiness and purity are without doubt, her simplicity, humility, and humanity are perhaps open to question. As an example of the monastic existence, she invites comparison with the monk Ambrosius, and it seems to me that she suffers by that comparison. Ambrosius, who is celibate and to some degree ascetic, seems more humble and simple and his work is in the world, whatever his vocation. He reads some in ancient books, but his habit is to

> '. . . mingle with our folk;
> And knowing every honest face of theirs
> As well as ever shepherd knew his sheep,
> And every homely secret in their hearts,
> Delight myself with gossip and old wives,
> And ills and aches, and teethings, lyings-in,
> And mirthful sayings, children of the place,
> That have no meaning half a league away:
> Or lulling random squabbles when they rise,
> Chafferings and chatterings at the market-cross,
> Rejoice, small man, in this small world of mine,
> Yea, even in their hens and in their eggs—.' (549–60)

Because he lives "like an old badger in his earth, / With earth about him everywhere, despite / All fast and penance" (628–30), he is certainly different from the nun, who "prayed and fasted, till the sun / Shone, and the wind blew, through her" (98–99). And yet his pastoral existence strikes the reader as not less holy, only more human.

Women have not lost their influence in the kingdom and there can be little question that that of the nun is disastrous. Galahad, for all his spirituality, is lost to the kingdom. Percivale, for all his purity, "Cares but to pass into the silent life." Lancelot, whose motivation to the quest is at least partly selfish, as he hopes to cleanse himself of his sin, or more properly perhaps to cleanse himself so that he can cease sinning, is not so cleansed. Bors alone of the knights who return is unselfishly motivated in his quest. It is he "Who scarce had prayed or asked it for [himself]" (688) and would gladly have given up the sight of the grail if Lancelot could see it.[27]

27. See 648–56. Bors' great love and selflessness are suggested by the pelican on his casque, and it is Bors alone who escapes the censure of Arthur (see 753–54).

The Holy Grail has long been seen by critics to be the turning point in the fortunes of the Round Table, but I believe it marks an acceleration in the moral and social degeneration which had not begun, but had been for the first time certain in *Lancelot and Elaine.* With the death of spirit in the kingdom, the search for spirit turns disastrously outward—to the grail. Social purpose is lost sight of in the pursuit of individual salvation, and a sick world, it is hoped, will be healed by a kind of magic rather than by human effort. Individual redemption remains possible for Lancelot and Guinevere, but there is really no possibility after *Lancelot and Elaine* for the reformation of society; *The Holy Grail* is simply an inevitable step in the inexorable movement toward chaos. And in that movement from here forward the influence of women is consistently maleficent.

Pelleas and Ettare, the next book of "The Round Table," initiates the corruption of innocence which the following book, *The Last Tournament,* completes, as we move from the "Tournament of Youth" to the "Tournament of the Dead Innocence." The pattern of degeneration of the kingdom, as we saw, ironically reverses the pattern of generation: the nation, which had moved from its birth with the coming of Arthur, through the youth of Gareth to maturity, now moves from maturity through the corruption of youth in *Pelleas and Ettare* to dead infancy in *The Last Tournament.* And in that corruption Lynette, who had been the trial of faith which had proved Gareth, becomes Ettare, the trial of faith which destroys Pelleas, and the bestiality from which Arthur delivers the people in *The Coming of Arthur* returns in the imagery of the later books.

Pelleas at the beginning of the idyll is much like the young Gareth: as he approaches the court of Arthur, he smells of the fields and brings the sunshine with him (5–6). He knows "All that belongs to knighthood" and he loves (8), the two ingredients necessary to both social service and individual salvation. He loves, though the object of his love is yet unknown to him; he trusts, however, that she is as fair and pure as Guinevere (42). Pelleas' innocence allows him to believe in love and in the first principle of knighthood, that "Man's word is God in man." But his innocence is corrupted as he finds that all is false: Ettare lies to him and breaks his faith in love; Gawain lies to him and breaks his faith in knighthood. When he finds that Guinevere is faithless, all trust in the principle of love is broken and he forsakes the principle of knighthood represented by Arthur.

The terrible effect of Ettare on Pelleas is obvious, but she is only a more virulent form of a disease which is spreading throughout the kingdom. The disease is shared, for example, by Guinevere and the moral kinship of the two women is therefore suggested in a number of ways in the idyll. For example, Tennyson emphasizes through repetition (42, 512) their kinship in Pelleas' ironic wish to find a love as pure as Guinevere. Both Guinevere and Ettare are also essentially flesh: as we saw, Guinevere is initially described as "fairest of all flesh on earth." When Pelleas first sees Ettare, we are told that "The beauty of her flesh abashed the boy" (74). The fleshliness of the two women is rendered in the poem through the rose image, which is significantly associated with both women. As we saw, Guinevere associates herself with the rose in *Balin and Balan,* and in *Pelleas and Ettare* the association is reaffirmed: when Gawain sings his song about the rose, we are told that it was a song Pelleas heard "sung before the Queen" (388). Similarly Ettare's "bloom" is described as "A rosy dawn kindled in stainless heavens" (68), and the garden in which the pavillions are pitched and in which Pelleas finds Ettare and Gawain is a rose garden—

> . . . a slope of garden, all
> Of roses white and red, and brambles mixt
> And overgrowing them . . .
> Here too, all hushed below the mellow moon,
> Save that one rivulet from a tiny cave
> Came lightening downward, and so spilt itself
> Among the roses, and was lost again. (412–18) [28]

Finally the song which Gawain sings and Pelleas hears about the worm within the rose (391–400) surely has application alike to Guinevere and Ettare.[29]

The kingdom has not, however, reached its ultimate decay in

28. There is neither a garden nor any roses in Malory.

29. It is important that it is the worm within the rose, not the rose itself, which causes the death of him who loves the rose. Tennyson is not apparently denying the flesh, but discovering the corruption to which it is liable.

Pelleas and Ettare. It is true that there is a return to the bestiality
of *The Coming of Arthur* and that a darkness descends at the end
of the idyll. It is also true that the "life and use and name and
fame" which Merlin desired have become in Pelleas "wrath and
shame and hate and evil fame" (556). But guilt is still individual,
though spreading. And Ettare, corrupt as she is, is not without
some self-knowledge and virtue, which perhaps needed strength
from example. She feels some compassion for Pelleas and senses
her own inadequacy:

> 'Why have I pushed him from me? this man loves,
> If love there be: yet him I loved not. Why?
> I deemed him fool? yea, so? or that in him
> A something—was it nobler than myself?—
> Seemed my reproach? He is not of my kind.
> He could not love me, did he know me well.'
>
> (299–304) [30]

That the kingdom has not reached the final corruption, which
lies in the future, is made clear in the concluding lines of *Pelleas
and Ettare.* It is there that Lancelot and Guinevere "each foresaw
the dolorous day to be," and Mordred "thought, 'The time is hard
at hand.'" Mordred is certainly right as the culmination of the
decline of the kingdom comes in *The Last Tournament,* the
ninth book of "The Round Table."

In *Pelleas and Ettare,* as we saw, guilt was still individual,
though pervasive; in *The Last Tournament* guilt is general.
There is still good in the realm in Dagonet and in Arthur, but
there is no longer innocence. As the fool says, " 'The dirty nurse,
Experience, in her kind / Hath fouled me' " (317–18). And even
Arthur, though rather belatedly, begins to suspect:

> . . . 'Is it then so well?
> Or mine the blame that oft I seem as he
> Of whom was written, "A sound is in his ears"?
> The foot that loiters, bidden go,—the glance
> That only seems half-loyal to command,—

30. The suggestion that Ettare eventually came to love Pelleas and wasted and
pined for him in vain is treated ambiguously by Tennyson. The poet asserts that he
who tells the tale says so, but in fact such a conclusion to Ettare's life does not
appear in Malory. Tennyson may be foreshadowing a like repentance in Guinevere.

A manner somewhat fallen from reverence—
Or have I dreamed the bearing of our knights
Tells of a manhood ever less and lower?
Or whence the fear lest this my realm, upreared,
By noble deeds at one with noble vows,
From flat confusion and brute violences,
Reel back into the beast, and be no more?'   (114–25)

In the loss of innocence and the subsequent corruption of the realm, all that is false is seen as a mockery of the true. Thus the general pattern of reversal established in *Pelleas and Ettare*, of degeneration as the exact opposite of generation, is followed. What had brought the kingdom to greatness is now reversed and as Arthur later says, " 'the loathsome opposite / Of all my heart had destined did obtain' " (*Guinevere*, 488–89).

There are numerous examples of the mockery of the true by the false. For example, the fool is set up by Gawain as a "mock-knight of Arthur's Table Round" (2). The last tournament, which was to commemorate the death of the innocent "Nestling," we are told, is "By these in earnest those in mockery called / The Tournament of the Dead Innocence" (135–36). It is a mockery because it celebrates not only the death of the dead innocent, but the death of all innocence. And Lancelot as mock umpire sits in judgment of a tourney in which all "the laws that ruled the tournament [are] / Broken" (160–61). That Lancelot should preside at the tourney and sit in Arthur's chair is a further mockery in that it publicly reflects Lancelot's secret usurpation of Arthur's role as husband. Guinevere's hope that the carcanet, prize of the tournament, will be won by "the purest of thy knights . . . for the purest of my maids" (49–50) ironically comes true. It is won by Tristram for Isolt, for with the death of Elaine and the corruption of Pelleas none are apparently any purer than Tristram and Isolt. Even the love triangle of Mark, Tristram, and Isolt is a terrible parodic mockery of that of Arthur, Lancelot, and Guinevere.[31] All that *is* in the kingdom is a hideous mockery of what should be.

31. Tristram seems clearly to recognize the parodic nature of his relationship to Isolt, as Isolt says,

'Ah then, false hunter and false harper, thou
Who brakest through the scruple of my bond,

All along, of course, there has been the heathen threat from without the kingdom. Gradually, as we have seen, the corruption and bestiality from without have permeated the fabric of the kingdom itself. The ultimate in degeneration is reached when corruption is freely chosen, when bestiality, unfaithfulness, and the lie are no longer the sporadic results of weakness within the realm, but have become the results of free moral choice. Where in *Pelleas and Ettare* the maddened Pelleas found Ettare's castle to be a harlot roof and her heart to be a harlot's heart (457, 459), he did not choose that it be so. But in *The Last Tournament* the Red Knight establishes his "Round Table of the North," in parody of Arthur's, on harlotry and adultery as knightly principles. Moreover, the vow, which has been so sacred to Arthur, is used to bind the northern knights to principles opposite to Arthur's (79–88). In order to gauge adequately the extent of degeneration of the realm it is important to remember that the "Round Table of the North" is not established by a heathen but by one of Arthur's own disenchanted knights (perhaps Pelleas) and is ultimately the result, therefore, of corruption not from without, but from within the kingdom.

Both Tristram and Isolt, around whom the action finally centers in *The Last Tournament,* also freely and in knowledge of what they are doing choose the false rather than the true. Isolt, for example, though she clearly recognizes that Tristram has "grown wild beast" (632), chooses him. And though it has been established throughout the *Idylls* that "Man's word is God in man," she freely and knowingly chooses the lie rather than the truth. She says,

'. . . I should suck
Lies like sweet wines: lie to me: I believe.
Will ye not lie? not swear, as there ye kneel,
And solemnly as when ye sware to him,
The man of men, our King—My God, the power
Was once in vows when men believed the King!
They lied not then, who sware, and through their vows

Calling me thy white hind, and saying to me
That Guinevere had sinned against the highest,
And I—misyoked with such a want of man—
That I could hardly sin against the lowest.' (563–68)

> The King prevailing made his realm:—I say,
> Swear to me thou wilt love me even when old,
> Gray-haired, and past desire, and in despair.' (639–48)

Tristram makes a similar choice. In his song there is a clear
recognition of the distinction between the false and the true,
between the shadow and the reality:

> 'Ay, ay, O ay—the winds that bend the brier!
> A star in heaven, a star within the mere!
> Ay, ay, O ay—a star was my desire,
> And one was far apart, and one was near:
> Ay, ay, O ay—the winds that bow the grass!
> And one was water and one star was fire,
> And one will ever shine and one will pass.
> Ay, ay, O ay—the winds that move the mere.' (725–32)

Obviously Tristram chooses the reflection in the mere, the water
rather than the fire, what will pass rather than what will ever
shine. In choosing what was near rather than what was far apart
he has chosen the shadow rather than the reality, and he has done
so freely and in full knowledge of his action. The ultimate corruption has therefore come both to the individual and the kingdom when knowingly the lie is preferred to truth, unfaith to
faith, disobedience to obedience, the shadow to reality.

By the end of *The Last Tournament* the kingdom and the
individual alike have gone through the inevitable disintegration
to which all nations and all individuals are subject. As the flesh
is liable to dissolution, so is the life of the nation. The nation
itself must pass, but new nations will be born which will have the
potential at least to further the spiritual advance of universal
history as Arthur's kingdom has done. Arthur's kingdom cannot
be reformed. It has passed inevitably over into a new barbarity,
but the individual can be redeemed through repentance. It is
here that the nation and the individual part, as the nation has
completed its cycle on the lower plane of the natural world where
all is cyclical. But though the cycle of the individual is similar on
the lower plane, that is, from birth to death, the individual can
transcend the cycle through spiritual rebirth.

The final book of "The Round Table," *Guinevere,* concentrates not on the further corruption of the kingdom, but on the singular contribution to that corruption made by the Queen and her repentance for her actions. A contrite Guinevere has been brought to realize her significant role in the destruction of the Arthurian ideals, those ideals which Arthur enumerates for her:

> 'To reverence the King, as if he were
> Their conscience, and their conscience as their King,
> To break the heathen and uphold the Christ,
> To ride abroad redressing human wrongs,
> To speak no slander, no, nor listen to it,
> To honour his own word as if his God's,
> To lead sweet lives in purest chastity,
> To love one maiden only, cleave to her,
> And worship her by years of noble deeds,
> Until they won her. . . .' (465–74)

Arthur, in a rather self-righteous tone of moral superiority which is at once priggish and quite human, makes Guinevere's culpability paramount, for he recognizes the degree to which man's right action hinges on the influence of women:

> '. . . for indeed I knew
> Of no more subtle master under heaven
> Than is the maiden passion for a maid,
> Not only to keep down the base in man,
> But teach high thought, and amiable words
> And courtliness, and the desire of fame,
> And love of truth, and all that makes a man.' (474–80)

Arthur's judgment of Guinevere's contribution to social disintegration is a judgment in which Guinevere herself concurs; she says of herself, " 'Ye know me then, that wicked one, who broke / The vast design and purpose of the King' " (663–64). We are not, of course, to hold Guinevere alone responsible for the destruction of the kingdom, but the focus of the final book of "The Round Table" on Guinevere at least suggests the centrality of the theme of woman's role in society which has been traced in this chapter.

The kingdom, of course, is irredeemably lost by the time of

Guinevere, but individual redemption, as I have said, is still possible. Lancelot's redemption does not occur in Guinevere, but we are told of it at the end of *Lancelot and Elaine,* where Lancelot in "remorseful pain" is unaware that "he should die a holy man." Guinevere's redemption is similar: she goes through recognition and repentance to salvation. She sees that it was her duty, as it would have been her pleasure and profit, to have loved the highest, yet her pride caused her to look not up but down (635–56). She has come to recognize that Arthur is "the highest and most human too" (644), as he is most spiritual. Though the flesh is necessary, Lancelot and Guinevere have chosen it exclusively and rejected spirit, and that is the sin for which they must repent.[32] Guinevere's salvation comes through her recognition of the primacy of the spirit, her sincere repentance, and her development of the capacity for spiritual love. She therefore finally passes "To where beyond these voices there is peace" (692).

*

The tendency of modern audiences is, I think, to concur with Sterling's criticism of the *Idylls,* that "The miraculous legend of 'Excalibar,' does not come very near to us, and as reproduced by any modern writer must be a mere ingenious exercise of fancy." And yet clearly Tennyson does not attempt to "reproduce" the legend of Excalibar. Nor is he trying, I think, to restore a decayed medievalism. What is archaic, or perhaps obsolete, about the *Idylls of the King* is not its Arthurian material. It is the ideas of the poem or, perhaps more properly, the ideals of the poem which fail to speak to the modern world.

In order to preserve those values which he saw endangered in the Victorian world, Tennyson attempted to teach the historical lesson of the generation and degeneration of a society in which the virtues of truth, obedience, faithfulness, and courtesy became corrupted. That alone would not have made the *Idylls* uncongenial to the modern temper, but Tennyson's attempt to preserve for woman her traditional role as complement rather than equal of man cast him on the losing side in the most revolutionary battle of the nineteenth century—the fight for women's rights.

32. Arthur makes this clear (548–65).

There can be little question that the traditional role of women was under strong attack at least as early as Mary Wollstonecraft's *Rights of Women* (1792),[33] and John Killham has shown in *Tennyson and "The Princess"* to what extent Tennyson was both familiar with and concerned about the "the woman question." It is, I submit, Tennyson's answer to that question perhaps more than anything else which makes the *Idylls* seem antiquated. A world which produced a Sue Bridehead could hardly be expected to accept, or perhaps even to understand, an Enid or an Elaine.

If the *Idylls* fails to speak to the modern world, then, that failure is the result to a great degree of Tennyson's attempt to preserve a lost and perhaps ultimately indefensible ideal of womanhood.[34] And yet one might argue in Tennyson's defense that though he finally failed to provide for the emergent "new woman" a role satisfactory to her, neither has anyone else been able to do so. At any rate, the appeal which the chivalric ideals of knighthood and the power of women for good made to the poet, disenchanted with his own age, must have been great, but for the modern reader the *Idylls* has perhaps little more attraction than the medieval romances of Scott. Tennyson's fight for an ideal womanhood, a fight which was lost in the nineteenth century, may well seem irrelevant in the twentieth.

33. For a discussion of the importance of *Vindication of the Rights of Women,* see Maurice J. Quinlan, "The Model Female," *Victorian Prelude* (New York, 1941), pp. 139–59.

34. Even to contemporaries, Tennyson's vision of woman apparently seemed remote, for example Joseph Jacobs (*Tennyson and "In Memoriam,"* p. 13): "But his whole conception of Guinevere, and still more of Vivien, was that of the nineteenth-century English gentleman, and something in the spirit of Mr. Podsnap."

7. Some Later Poems

*T*HE later poems of Tennyson, those roughly from 1860 until his death (excluding the *Idylls*), tend to be short (with the exception of *Enoch Arden,* a rather dull poem by modern standards but immensely popular in its day).[1] These include, as one would expect, poems highly successful and those considerably less so. There are the necessary occasional poems of the poet laureate; dramatic monologues of pre-Christian figures such as Tiresias, Lucretius, Demeter, and the Ancient Sage or of Christian figures such as Sir John Oldcastle and Columbus; monologues of English bucolic characters, which include some fine poems such as *The Northern Farmer: Old Style* in a genre new to Tennyson—dialect poetry. There are themes of the earlier poetry renewed: poems of the spiritual quest, of the love of the good woman, of nationalism, of the battle of soul and sense. There are also some rather cranky poems which rail at the ills of the age or bemoan the ephemeral nature of poetic fame.

Space does not allow an examination of all the poems of the last three decades of Tennyson's life, nor are all the poems worth the attention. I have therefore in a wholly arbitrary manner divided into three groups the poems which I wish to treat: (1) pre-Christian monologues—*The Ancient Sage, Demeter and Persephone, Lucretius;* (2) Christian monologues—*Sir John Oldcastle, Lord Cobham* and *Columbus;* (3) speculative poems—*The Voyage of Maeldune, De Profundis, The Higher Pantheism,* and *Flower in the Crannied Wall.*[2]

1. I have not, of course, included here Tennyson's plays, written in verse between 1875 and 1884.

2. It will be noted that I have chosen not to deal with some very good poems, most notably *The Northern Farmer: Old Style* and *Rizpah. The Northern Farmer:*

By labeling the first group of poems pre-Christian I mean no more than that the speakers of them lived in ages before Christ; therefore one should perhaps not expect the metaphysical problems and solutions with which they deal to be uniquely Christian. And yet Tennyson's apparent belief in the eternal presence of Christ [3] and in the principle of accommodation as it operates in a progressive religion suggests to me at least that pre-Christian need not necessarily mean non-Christian; that is, *The Ancient Sage*, for example, may be a Christian poem in the sense that Browning's *Saul* is a Christian poem, although the speaker in each case antedates Christ.[4]

The metaphysical speculations which take place in a pre-Christian world in *The Ancient Sage* (1885) are not radically different from those which appear in earlier Tennyson poems in Christian contexts. Because the natural world is the diverse manifestation of spiritual unity, because it is the shadow which at once reveals and hides a higher reality, faith in the spirit is possible to the individual in the pre-Christian as well as in the post-Christian world. In other words, the natural world is our means to that wisdom which perceives the spirit. In *In Memoriam*, for example, the persona was able to recognize Christ's eternal presence through its manifestation in Arthur Hallam. The persona, through his knowledge of Hallam, arrives at the wisdom which perceives Christ, though Christ remains inaccessible to his knowledge. In *The Ancient Sage* the same wisdom is affirmed by the sage. When the young man in his poem, the "deathsong for the Ghouls" (17), from which the sage reads, maintains that

---

Old Style (1864), the best of the dialect poems, is an admirable study of the conservative values and self-respect of nineteenth-century yeomanry. *Rizpah* (1880) as a study in madness shows that Tennyson had not lost his touch since *Maud*.

3. See *The Ancient Sage*, for example: "But louder than thy rhyme the silent Word / Of that world-prophet in the heart of man" (212–13). The capitalization of the *Word* suggests that Christ is present to the sage, who antedates Christ by a thousand years.

4. It can be argued, of course, that *The Ancient Sage* is strictly neither pre-Christian nor a monologue. It opens with an introduction establishing the time of the whole poem as post-Christian and the form as narration rather than monologue: "A thousand summers ere the time of Christ / From out his ancient city came a Seer." But the body of the poem after the initial eight lines is in the voice of the sage, who carries on a dialogue with himself as he reads and responds to the young man's poem.

"The nameless never came / Among us, never spake with man, / And never named the Name" (54–56), he means that God has not become incarnate and therefore we can have no knowledge of him. But men can have no *knowledge* of God whether or not he becomes incarnate; though God reveals himself in the flesh, he also hides himself in the flesh and therefore requires for his acceptance the same act of faith which the sage recommends. The young man accurately asserts that " 'The nameless Power, or Powers, that rule / Were never heard or seen,' " (29–30), but that fact simply makes necessary the sage's distinction between knowledge and wisdom, a distinction similar to that made by the persona of *In Memoriam* (CXIV) ; the sage says,

> . . . the Nameless hath a voice,
> By which thou wilt abide, if thou be wise,
> As if thou knewest, though thou canst not know;
> . . . .
> For nothing worthy proving can be proven,
> Nor yet disproven: wherefore thou be wise,
> Cleave ever to the sunnier side of doubt,
> And cling to Faith beyond the forms of Faith!
> (34–36, 66–69)

For the young man, just as for the persona of *In Memoriam*, trust in the Nameless requires the power to believe where we cannot prove.

Not only is the wisdom which perceives God in *The Ancient Sage* of the same kind as that in *In Memoriam*, but the way to that wisdom is the same for the sage as it had been for the persona: it is through the faculty of feeling rather than the faculty of reason, which deals alone with knowledge. The Power perceived by wisdom and the faculty for its perception are described by the sage:

> . . . That which knows,
> And is not known, but felt through what we feel
> Within ourselves is highest, shall descend
> On this half-deed, and shape it at the last
> According to the Highest in the Highest.   (86–90)

The Power differs little from "The Power in darkness whom we guess" of *In Memoriam* (CXXIV) and the faculty for its perception is essentially the same as in *In Memoriam*.[5]

More important perhaps than the way in which wisdom reaches us, that is, through feeling rather than through reason, is what that wisdom tells us. And here again wisdom perceives the same truth that it had perceived in *In Memoriam*. The persona of *In Memoriam* learned that the apparent antinomies of the phenomenal world could be reconciled through a trust in the spiritual unity behind the world. In *The Ancient Sage* the same conclusion is reached: the apparent contradictions of life are the result of "This double seeming of the single world!" (105). When the young man argues,

> 'For all that laugh, and all that weep,
>   And all that breathe are one
> Slight ripple on the boundless deep
>   That moves, and all is gone.'

the sage answers,

> But that one ripple on the boundless deep
> Feels that the deep is boundless, and itself
> For ever changing form, but evermore
> One with the boundless motion of the deep.   (191–94)

As the persona of *In Memoriam* came to recognize, it is only the form which changes and must change. Change is the surface of permanence as diversity is the manifestation of unity. It is this which the sage perceives when he suggests that it is "As if the late and early were but one" (222); it is this perception behind his remark that the "Day and Night are children of the Sun" (245). If the world seems double, it is single nonetheless.

The Ancient Sage echoes not only some of the conclusions reached in *In Memoriam*, but conclusions reached in other earlier

5. Cf.

> A warmth within the breast would melt
>   The freezing reason's colder part,
>   And like a man in wrath the heart
> Stood up and answered 'I have felt.'   (CXXIV)

poems as well. The experience of Galahad, for example, is essentially repeated in the sage, who says,

> . . . for more than once when I
> Sat all alone, revolving in myself
> The word that is the symbol of myself,
> The mortal limit of the Self was loosed,
> And past into the Nameless, as a cloud
> Melts into Heaven. I touched my limbs, the limbs
> Were strange not mine—and yet no shade of doubt,
> But utter clearness, and through loss of Self
> The gain of such large life as matched with ours
> Were Sun to spark—unshadowable in words,
> Themselves but shadows of a shadow-world.   (229–39)

When in *The Holy Grail* Galahad cries, "If I lose myself, I save myself," he is, of course, paraphrasing Matthew 10:39 and speaking of the salvation of his soul. But for both Galahad and the sage, the act of losing oneself is a mystical experience. There is a difference, however, between Galahad and the sage. Galahad is not, as we saw, without censure for his pursuit of the mystical experience because he left the wrongs of the world to right themselves: as Arthur says of Galahad, " 'his chair desires him here in vain, / However they may crown him otherwhere' " (897–98) . The sage is not to be censured, on the other hand, because apparently he has, like Ulysses, fulfilled his responsibilities to the world; he is extremely old and has, as we are told, only one more year to live. It is important to recognize that he is ancient if his abandonment to mysticism is to be seen as legitimate. He does not, for example, counsel mysticism for the young, but counsels service. The young man is advised to return to the city to "help thy fellow men" (258) , to live, like Arthur's knights, a life of use. Tennyson asserts again here the necessity for life in the world, as he had in *The Palace of Art, The Lotos-Eaters, The Holy Grail,* and other places; it is only the ancient sage, wearied of the city, who is allowed to spend his one remaining year among the hills. In *The Ancient Sage* of 1885 old themes are renewed and Tennyson sums up and happily blends ideas which he had held as early as 1833.

   Demeter and Persephone, the best of the poems in the volume of 1889, *Demeter, and Other Poems,* has been variously interpreted by critics. Jerome Buckley suggests that "it is the burden of the idyl to demonstrate that love can restore the self and so transcend the force of death and hell." [6] E. D. H. Johnson reads the poem as a study of the Tennysonian creative process: "Persephone, appearing in dream, explains that her periodic withdrawal from the phenomenal world to the nether region of shadows does not really involve a loss, but is mysteriously necessitated by the process of creation. . . . When interpreted in this way, *Demeter and Persephone* becomes a symbolic representation of Tennyson's entire poetic career. Beneath his artistic productivity lay dark depths of consciousness on communion with which, rather than on any external stimulus, depended his will to create." [7] G. Robert Stange, in the most extended study of the poem, is in partial agreement with Johnson: "The most striking achievement of the poem is the consistency with which the language of myth is used to include reflections on the nature of artistic creation, on the condition of the age, and on religious doctrine." [8] Stange's perceptive reading of the poem is admirably qualified by James Kissane, whose study of Victorian mythology and the " 'three phase' notion of mythological interpretation" is used to clarify the poem.[9] Because both Stange and Kissane have so effectively analyzed the first two phases of mythological interpretation in the poem—response to nature and human story—I will limit my remarks to the third phase—spiritual insight— though even here I wish only to add what is perhaps a further dimension to Kissane's reading of the fourth section of the poem.

The final paragraph, critics agree, contains Tennyson's mod-

6. *Tennyson*, p. 246.

7. *Alien Vision*, p. 66.

8. "Tennyson's Mythology: A Study of *Demeter and Persephone*," p. 140. Stange finds the poem most successful in its reflections on artistic creation, less so on religious doctrine.

9. "Victorian Mythology," *Victorian Studies*, 6 (1962) : 5–28. The three phases are derived from Walter Pater's *Greek Studies*, particularly "A Study of Dionysus" (1876) and "The Myth of Demeter and Persephone" (1876) : "In his essay on Demeter, Pater interprets the myth at the primitive stage, in which it expresses 'impressions of the phenomena of the natural world,' as embodying the process of seasonal growth, decay, and regeneration. Its 'conscious, poetical, or literary phase' focused upon the mother-daughter relationship and the emotions it engenders. Finally, the myth in its most spiritualized form transfigures these emotions and their accompanying incidents into the promise of a life to come" (Kissane, pp. 25–26) .

ernization of the old myth. It is here that Demeter perceives
" 'Fate beyond the Fates' " and asks what is that Fate

> But younger kindlier Gods to bear us down,
> As we bore down the Gods before us? Gods,
> To quench, not hurl the thunderbolt, to stay,
> Not spread the plague, the famine; Gods indeed,
> To send the noon into the night and break
> The sunless halls of Hades into Heaven?
> Till thy dark lord accept and love the Sun,
> And all the Shadow die into the Light.   (129–36)

It is here that the spiritual insight, beyond the response to nature
and human story, appears.

Kissane has this to say of the "ethical" theme of the poem as a
whole: "The 'ethical' theme and the human situation are con-
veyed through the details of the nature myth. Moreover, the
theme of immortality is not simply imposed upon the portrayal of
emotion; it rises out of it. The dominant emotion is love, involved in grief yet transcending it; and love, in a number of
ways, lies at the heart of those intimations of immortality which
the poem glimpses. It is first of all Demeter's consuming love
which wins life for her daughter. Again, that same love underlies
her 'ill-content' and her consequent hope in 'kindlier Gods' and in
Death's overthrow. Appropriately then this new dispensation is
envisioned in terms of love: an indifferent deity supplanted by a
God of Love who will be worshipped not fearfully but lovingly.
The conception is basically that which informs *In Memoriam*:
the survival of love beyond death sustains faith in eternal life and
defines God's nature as 'Immortal Love.' " [10] I certainly agree with
such an interpretation, but I would go beyond either Stange or
Kissane to suggest the specifically Christian overtones of the poem
and what they tell us about the theme.[11]

10. P. 28.
11. Stange grants that "The myth of Persephone has been reinterpreted as an
anticipation of the story of Christ," but he concludes that "The success of Tennyson's reinterpretation is not . . . an unqualified one" (p. 149). In commenting on
the lines "Till thy dark lord accept and love the Sun, / And all the Shadow die
into the Light," Kissane says, "This may be seen, from the poem's pagan perspective, as an anticipation of the Christian dispensation; but it is more the expression,
in his own peculiar accents of evolutionism, of Tennyson's dim yet emotion-tinged

Demeter, like David in Browning's *Saul*, seems to intuit a God of Love from her own love for Persephone, as David had intuited such a God from his love for Saul. Both Demeter and David, of course, antedate Christ, the God of Love, but the means to a recognition of the divine nature as Love are available alike to pre-Christian and post-Christian humanity. It is for David and Demeter a human relationship which leads to the prophetic recognition of a God of Love, but in both cases the poets suggest through the imagery that we associate the object of the speaker's love with Christ even before that recognition comes. In other words, the imagery which surrounds Persephone, like the imagery which surrounds Saul, is imagery normally associated with Christ. Persephone, like Saul, therefore, can be seen to anticipate, to prefigure, the God of Love which she promises.[12]

Persephone is described, for example, as "human-godlike" (19) just as Christ of the Prologue to *In Memoriam* "seemest human and divine." She is, moreover, "The Life that had descended" which "re-arise[s]" (30), and is described as "having risen from out the dead" (142). Not only does she herself re-arise, but she has the power of life: when her foot touches it, the "blank earth-baldness clothes itself afresh, / And breaks into the crocus-purple hour" (49–50). As we have seen, this is the same image that Tennyson had used to describe Maud's power to resurrect— as the hero says that though he had lain for a century dead, the touch of Maud's foot would cause his dust to "blossom in purple and red" (I, 923). And it is essentially the same image used to describe Christ's similar power in the Prologue to *In Memoriam*.[13] Persephone is also lighted by the Sun (31), that Sun which her dark Lord will eventually come to accept and love when "all the Shadow [shall] die into the Light" (135–36). Here Tennyson may be employing the Sun–Son pun of *Christus Oriens* tradition. At any rate, Tennyson's image of the shadow which dies into light employs the most common metaphor of typological exegesis to describe the operation of prefiguration and recapitulation. That

---

personal faith in that 'one far-off divine event / To which the whole creation moves' " (p. 27).

12. For my defense of Saul as theological type in Browning, see "Time and Type in Browning's *Saul*," *ELH*, 33 (1966): 370–89.

13. See above, pp. 81–82.

is, the shadow both prefigures and promises the reality, which is Christ, who of course is the Light.

The association of Persephone with Christ through the imagery of the poem is not meant to suggest that she *is* Christ or that she is a symbol of Christ. She is the quite human reality which prefigures and promises the greater reality, a God of Love. Persephone is no less "real" than Arthur Hallam or Maud and she is, like them, the means to spiritual wisdom. We see, therefore, not only the real Persephone, but through the imagery of the poem the greater reality behind her, and that greater reality is not only present in the incarnation but is eternally present and perceptible to us through our love for other human beings.

What is important about recognizing the relationship between Persephone and Christ in the poem is that it leads to a clearer recognition of Tennyson's belief in a progressive religion. God is continually at work in the world and the means to perceive him according to our light are continually available to us. The spiritual is reflected in the natural—in a Hallam, a Maud, or a Persephone—have we but the love which leads to the wisdom necessary for its perception. Christ is eternally present both in those who prefigure and promise him and those whom Hopkins called AfterChrists, those who come after and reflect him. Such a belief on Tennyson's part quite accords with traditional Christianity and is more, I think, than an example of "Tennyson's dim yet emotion-tinged personal faith in that 'one far-off divine event / To which the whole creation moves.' "

Lucretius (1868) is the last of the poems grouped here as pre-Christian monologues. Commentary on the poem has been varied: it has been read both as an effort to compete with Swinburne on his own ground and as an answer to Swinburne; [14] it has been read as an expression of Tennyson's "mood of introspective depression," [15] and as a demonstration of "the inadequacy of even the highest naturalistic philosophy to provide an incentive for either the humane life or the arts that embody humanity's aspiration." [16] Certainly the poem is in part at least about the inadequacy of a naturalistic philosophy. It is also, as Jerome Buckley has pointed

14. See Buckley's refutation of these charges in *Tennyson*, p. 168 and *n*.
15. Johnson, *Alien Vision*, p. 34.
16. Buckley, *Tennyson*, p. 168.

out, a distinctly Roman, as opposed to Greek, figure speaking from a Roman context.[17] In spite of this fact (or perhaps because of it) the subject matter of *Lucretius* and that of *Demeter and Persephone* are really, it seems to me, two halves of the same coin; that is, these "pre-Christian" poems are a negative and a positive reaction to faith through love. As we saw in *Demeter and Persephone*, Demeter's ability to love her daughter led to the spiritual wisdom which forecast a God of Love. In *Lucretius* we find in the Roman's inability to love a consequent spiritual enervation and suicide.

The poem opens with a statement of the fundamental inadequacy of Lucretius:

> Lucilia, wedded to Lucretius, found
> Her master cold; for when the morning flush
> Of passion and the first embrace had died
> Between them, though he loved her none the less,
> Yet often when the woman heard his foot
> Return from pacings in the field, and ran
> To greet him with a kiss, the master took
> Small notice, or austerely, for—his mind
> Half buried in some weightier argument,
> Or fancy-borne perhaps upon the rise
> And long roll of the Hexameter—he past
> To turn and ponder those three hundred scrolls
> Left by the Teacher, whom he held divine.   (1–13)

Lucretius, in a poem written at the time Tennyson was at work on *Idylls of the King*, is in some ways like King Arthur. As Arthur, incapable of joining with the flesh of Guinevere though he loved her, both made fruition impossible and brought, indirectly at least, death and destruction, so does Lucretius through a like incapacity do the same. It can be argued that Lucilia's love philtre is hardly the answer to her husband's neglect, and neither is Guinevere's adultery an answer, but one can grant the argument and yet insist upon the error of both Arthur and Lucretius. In

---

17. "The Roman subject invites and receives a more austere and less 'idyllic' treatment than the Greek legend of, say, Tithonus or the Hesperides; for Lucretius is placed in a society no longer open to wonder, but bent rather upon the total destruction of the imagination and the intellect" (*Tennyson*, p. 166).

rejecting his wife Lucretius has shut love out,[18] and thereby not only denies his wife completion but makes himself one-sided. That he has shut out love is suggested, I think, not only by his wife's distraction over his neglect, but also by his refusal to offer a dove or even a rose to the goddess of love, Venus (67–69). In shutting out love, Lucretius has, of course, lost the means to spiritual enlightenment.

Because Lucretius makes no place for love in his naturalistic philosophy, he is restricted to a world of phenomenal knowledge; he develops the power to believe only where he can prove. His inability to love sufficiently makes impossible the Tennysonian spiritual advance through the human relationship to the wisdom which perceives the "Unity of Nature, and the purpose hidden behind the cosmic process of matter in motion and changing forms of life."[19] The consequence of exalting knowledge to a quite undeserved supreme position[20] is that Lucretius is unprepared to deal with the fact that, as the Ancient Sage put it, "nothing worthy proving can be proven, / Nor yet disproven"; he cannot therefore "be wise, [and] / Cleave ever to the sunnier side of doubt" (66–68). Lucretius' dependence on knowledge rather than wisdom therefore causes him to deny the gods and commit suicide.

That phenomenal knowledge is not only inadequate but leads to false conclusions is most obvious in Lucretius' comment on his vision of the satyr: "but him I proved impossible; / Twy-natured is no nature" (193–94). It is precisely here where Lucretius is most wrong. What he means, as the Lucretius of the *De Rerum Natura* had meant, is that creatures half man and half beast like the satyr are impossible, though the narrator of the poem ironically informs us that Lucretius himself is half man and half beast when he speaks of the "brute brain within the man's" (21). More important than the irony is the fact that the "proof" of the impossibility of the satyr leads Lucretius to the absolute judgment that "twy-natured is no nature." Such a judgment rules out not only the possibility of the combination of beast and man, but also the combinations human and divine, flesh and spirit, male and

18. Though we are told that Lucretius loved Lucilia in spite of his neglect (4) he is, like Arthur, hardly a complement to his wife and can therefore, I think, be judged derelict in his role as husband through insufficient love.

19. *Memoir*, p. 270.

20. Cf. *In Memoriam* cxiv.

female—all of which are "twy-natured." Far from being no nature, twy-nature is the most complete nature. Ironically Lucretius ignores the opportunity to prove that twy-nature is complete nature when he neglects his marriage.

The unity of apparent contrarieties, of flesh and spirit, for example, or humanity and divinity, finds an analogue in the joining of man and wife (not of course because one is flesh and the other spirit, but because they are complementary and join to form one). As the hero of *The Princess* had said some twenty years earlier,

> '. . . either sex alone
> Is half itself, and in true marriage lies
> Nor equal, nor unequal: each fulfils
> Defect in each, and always thought in thought,
> Purpose in purpose, will in will, they grow,
> The single pure and perfect animal,
> The two-celled heart beating, with one full stroke,
> Life.'   (Part VII, 283–90)

If indeed the Prince is right (and there is considerable evidence that Tennyson shared the Prince's belief), then Lucretius is incomplete rather than "the single pure and perfect animal." He has, in denying his wife, ignored the evidence of harmony in a world apparently contrary. Not only is marriage a sign of the essential unity of a twy-natured world, but it is analogous to the harmonious relation of the male and female principles within the single complete soul. As Tennyson suggested in a short poem of 1889,

> While man and woman still are incomplete,
> I prize that soul where man and woman meet,
> Which types all Nature's male and female plan. . . .[21]

It is precisely this sort of twy-nature which Tennyson most highly prized in Christ, that is, "What he called 'the man-woman'

---

21. *On One Who Affected an Effeminate Manner*, published in *Demeter, and Other Poems*. Though this poem satirizes an individual, there is little doubt that Tennyson is serious in the lines quoted.

in Christ, the union of tenderness and strength"; [22] it is also the "manhood fused with female grace," which he attributed to Arthur Hallam in *In Memoriam* (CIX). Lucretius even identifies himself with Lucretia (235–42) as his female counterpart but ironically continues to ignore the essential twy-nature of "Nature's male and female plan." He therefore neglects the human relationship which alone leads to wisdom and is left with the appearance rather than the reality. Restricted to the phenomenal world of his naturalistic philosophy, Lucretius is left with despair and suicide.

*

The next group of poems—Christian monologues—includes *Sir John Oldcastle, Lord Cobham* (1880) and *Columbus* (1880). Both poems have generally suffered the neglect of anthologists and critics alike, and those critics who do deal briefly with them are usually condemnatory. Tennyson himself has perhaps contributed to the neglect of the poems in his comments upon them: of *Sir John Oldcastle* he said, " 'I took as subject of a poem . . . Sir John Oldcastle, Lord Cobham, because he is a fine historical figure' "; and of *Columbus*, " 'My poem of "Columbus" was founded on the following passage in Washington Irving's *Life of Columbus*.' " [23] Looked at merely as historical studies, the poems do perhaps recommend themselves to the following typical critical censure: "The two historical monologues . . . that appeared among the *Ballads* are quite as static as some of the principal scenes in the chronicle plays. . . . Neither piece really transcends the factual records out of which it is shaped." [24] But the poems are not, I think, merely historical, and they are better poems than they have generally been judged to be. Though *Columbus* apparently was an occasional poem, both poems seem to embody a

22. *Memoir*, p. 274n. Cf. the similar attribute in poets in the following lines from "Wherefore, in these dark ages of the press": "And if he be, as true-cast poets are, / Half woman-hearted, typing all his kind," or its variant "And if I be, as truecast Poets are, / Half woman-natured, typing all mankind" in Trinity Notebook 26 (c. 1839), printed in Christopher Ricks, "The Tennyson Manuscripts," p. 920.

23. *Memoir*, p. 630.

24. Buckley, *Tennyson*, pp. 217–18. Sir Charles Tennyson doesn't even mention either poem in his biography.

principle of progressive religion peculiarly relevant to the Victorian world.

Tennyson's choice of Oldcastle, the Wiclifite martyr burned as a heretic and traitor in 1417, was perhaps determined by Oldcastle's role in the defense of Wiclif's translation of the Bible. At any rate, in the poem the translation of the word becomes the central metaphor for the "translation" of the "Word." That is, the translation of the Latin gospel into English becomes a metaphor for the translation—transmission or transplantation—of the Word—Christ. Wiclif's translation of the word as it moves westward from the Latin of Rome to English and eventually to Welsh (22–23) even farther west is no more than the "Heaven-sweet Evangel," Paul, saw as fitting. Paul transplanted the Word from Greece in the East to Rome in the West by translating the gospel from Greek to Latin in his preaching. In a double sense then the Word must be continually "translated" westward.

Translation of the Bible into English or Welsh is only a part of the adaptability which religion must be capable of. Religion must also be capable of "translation" in the sense that culture is "translated" in the historic concept of the *translatio studii*. That is, as culture or studies had been seen to progress in a westward movement through their "translation," through their transference, by the adherents of the medieval and renaissance idea of *translatio studii*,[25] so is religion seen to progress through "translation" by the Liberal Anglicans. Such an idea of "translation" seems clearly to lie behind the following remarks by Stanley: "If the spirit of the original Christianity of Christ . . . is to be found not in the churches which sprang up on its native soil, but in churches more and more remote from those regions in climate, in feeling, in thought, it is because the spirit of the West, the conscience, the energy, the reason of the West, has broken the bonds which still fetter the older and more primitive, but not therefore necessarily the more Christian churches of the East. The Church of Rome is in this respect not only the witness against the exclusive claims of the Byzantine Church, but still more emphatically against her own. The Reformation was but another step in the same direc-

25. For an analysis of the *translatio studii* tradition and its use in "progress" poems of the seventeenth and eighteenth centuries, see Aubrey L. Williams, *Pope's Dunciad: A Study of Its Meaning* (London, 1955), pp. 44–48.

tion, to which the movements of Latin Christianity had already pointed the way." [26] In Tennyson's poem it is such an idea, I suggest, that is behind the "translation" of Bethlehem to Lutterworth and the apparent "translation" of Christ to Wiclif:

> Not least art thou, thou little Bethlehem
> In Judah, for in thee the Lord was born;
> Nor thou in Britain, little Lutterworth,
> Least, for in thee the word was born again.　(24–27)[27]

The westward progress of religion is also suggested when Oldcastle asks of Henry V,

> 　　　　　　　　Harry of Monmouth,
> Or Amurath of the East?
> 　　　　　　　　Better to sink
> Thy fleurs-de-lys in slime again, and fling
> Thy royalty back into the riotous fits
> Of wine and harlotry—thy shame, and mine,
> Thy comrade—than to persecute the Lord,
> And play the Saul that never will be Paul.　(92–98)

In borrowing Amurath, a Turkish Sultan, from Shakespeare, Tennyson is not asking us to relate Oldcastle to Falstaff. Oldcastle is asking whether Henry V will move forward as a Western Christian or backward toward Eastern heathenism.[28] It is clear that the movement toward the East is a degenerate one when such a movement is seen by Oldcastle as analogous to a return by Henry

26. Quoted in Forbes, p. 167n97. These remarks by Stanley appear in a review of Milman's *History of Latin Christianity* in the *Quarterly Review,* 95 (1854): 49–50.

27. Cf. the "translation" of paradise to England in *Maud*, Part I, section XVIII, verse iii. There the cedar of Lebanon is seen to have been transplanted to England from paradise, and in the West its limbs have "increased / Upon a pastoral slope as fair." The suggestion is that it now shades a new Eve—Maud.

28. Cf. Tennyson in *The Hesperides* (1832), "All good things are in the west"; or Coleridge in *Table Talk,* 1823: "Europeans and Orientalists may be well represented by two figures standing back to back: the latter looking to the East, that is, backwards; the former looking Westward, or forwards" (quoted in Forbes, p. 167n97). Or Stanley, "The Eastern Church was, like the East, stationary and immutable; the Western, like the West, progressive and flexible" (in Forbes, p. 84). Such an attitude toward the relative merits of East and West was pervasive in Tennyson's day.

to a youth of riot and waste; such a return would of course be a reversal of the natural process of growth.

The allusion to Saul elaborates the same idea: Saul, as a "Hellenist" Jew,[29] was capable of progress from the Hellenism and Judaism of the East to the Christianity of the West and thereby became Paul. Indeed, the Hebrew word *Saul* becomes in translation the Latin word *Paul*. Moreover, Paul's translation of the word from the Greek to Latin as he moves westward from the "soft Mediterranean shores" of Greece to "the Latin crowd" (30, 31) of Rome further exemplifies the necessity of "translation" westward in spiritual progress.[30]

Retrogression to heathenism or Judaism is not all that is rejected by Oldcastle, but also a static and inflexible contemporary Church. For the Liberal Anglicans "where there is no progress there must be decline,"[31] and Tennyson suggests the same in Oldcastle's denunciation of the superstitious practices of a reactionary Christianity. Oldcastle sees no efficacy in pilgrimages, confession, and absolution, the doctrine of transubstantiation, or the wooden cross. Indeed, Oldcastle uses the cross at once as itself and as metaphor for the dead wood of the Church:

> Here is the copse, the fountain and—a Cross!
> To thee, dead wood, I bow not head nor knees.
> Rather to thee, green boscage, work of God,
> Black holly, and white-flowered wayfaring-tree!
> Rather to thee, thou living water, drawn
> By this good Wiclif mountain down from heaven,
> And speaking clearly in thy native tongue—
> No Latin—He that thirsteth, come and drink!   (120–27)

29. See *Interpreter's Bible* (New York, 1954) , 9:118.

30. The Liberal Anglicans made much of translation of the Bible. "Of all books the Bible loses least of its force and dignity and beauty from being translated into other languages. . . . Moreover, as the Greek original belongs to a degenerate age of the language, and is tainted with many exoticisms and other defects, while our Version exhibits our language in its highest purity and majesty, in this respect it has a great advantage" (Hare, *Guesses at Truth: Second Series*, pp. 428–29) ; or "We are now so much accustomed to regard the Latin language as 'the tongue not understanded by the people,' and as a sign of all that is antiquated and obstructive to religious liberty, that we forget how completely this was reversed in the first beginning of its adoption by the Western Church" (Stanley, *Quarterly Review*, 95 [June and September 1854]:43) .

31. Forbes, p. 99.

Oldcastle rejects the dead wood in favor of the living tree and the living water, as he rejects the dead form in favor of the living presence. Because life requires and gives evidence for change, for growth, so must religion. To rigidify, as the Church had done, is to court death as the Gospel was "meant / To course and range through all the world," not to be "Tethered to these dead pillars of the Church" (113–15).

The modernism of *Sir John Oldcastle, Lord Cobham* lies in the fact that it celebrates a controversy very real for the Victorians. The crucial difference, I am convinced, between the Liberal Anglicans and the Oxford reformers led by Newman lay in their acceptance or rejection of the necessity for "translation," for transmission through growth and development of the Word. It was a young Newman's horror at the possibility of such a necessity which led him to see Liberalism as the Antichrist.[32] And though it was pretty clear by the end of the 1840s that the Liberal Anglicans had won their battle with the Oxford Movement, the controversy has remained and still remains in the twentieth century, as evidenced in the Vatican Councils of the 1960s.

Columbus, the second of the Christian monologues, was written, we are told, "after repeated entreaties from certain prominent Americans that [Tennyson] would commemorate the discovery of America in verse."[33] Ostensibly an occasional poem, it nevertheless seems to me thematically similar to *Sir John Oldcastle;* that is, it is also about the westward progress of religion. It is true that Columbus is not usually thought of as a religious figure like Oldcastle. And yet the idea of the discovery of America at a time when Tennyson was apparently working on *Sir John Oldcastle*[34] may have suggested to the poet similar thematic treatment.

32. Newman lists seventeen propositions he deems liberal which, while at Oxford, he "earnestly denounced and abjured." The seventh, though not seventh in importance, I think, is "Christianity is necessarily modified by the growth of civilization, and the exigencies of time" ("Note A, Liberalism," in *Apologia Pro Vita Sua,* ed. A. Dwight Culler [Riverside Edition, 1956], pp. 275–76). For a discussion of Newman's "theory of development" and the Liberal Anglican reaction to it, see Forbes, pp. 105–8.

33. *Memoir,* p. 631.

34. Both poems were published in *Ballads and Other Poems* (1880). Sir Charles Tennyson says that Tennyson had been working on the poems of this volume "intermittently for the past few months" (*Tennyson,* p. 454).

In spite of Columbus' praise of the Holy Church in the poem and his hope "to spread the Catholic faith" (226), it is clear that the Church in Spain is a force of reaction, not progress. In its inflexibility the Church has kept Columbus seven years in Spain defending his "golden guess" (42) of a spherical earth; it later allows its prelate Fonseca to send out Bovadilla to put Columbus in chains. And so Columbus says, "thus was I beaten back, / And chiefly to my sorrow by the Church" (54–55). The Church is wrong, not in its principles, from which Columbus says he has never swerved, "Not even by one hair's-breadth of heresy" (63), but because it has rigidified. David is not condemned for having "called the heavens a hide, a tent / Spread over earth, and so this earth was flat" (46–47); but a Church which does not progress beyond such a belief is wrong. Therefore Columbus insists that to disagree with David, Lactantius, and Augustine is not heretical; it is no more than to fulfill the prophecy of John: Columbus asks,

> Chains for the Admiral of the Ocean! chains
> For him who gave a new heaven, a new earth,
> As holy John had prophesied of me,
>
> . . . .
>
> Who pushed his prows into the setting sun,
> And made West East, and sailed the Dragon's mouth,
> And came upon the Mountain of the World,
> And saw the rivers roll from Paradise!   (19–21, 24–27)

Clearly Columbus sees his movement westward as ordained by God. It is in the West that a new heaven, a new earth, a new nature appear. Indeed Paradise is in the West, not East; it can be reached only by moving forward, not backward. That the westward movement of the poem is to be equated with spiritual progress is apparent through the allusion to the heavenly Jerusalem of Revelation. Man must press forward, westward, spiritually as he has progressed in knowledge since the time of David and Lactantius. In such a way are we to interpret Columbus' dream that "the Indian isle" is not San Salvador, "but our most ancient East / Moriah with Jerusalem" (79–80). The permanence of spiritual truth is manifested, not in its stasis, but in its repetition; we can find the "Mountain of the World" (called also the "Moun-

tain of Adam"), "Moriah," "Jerusalem," and "Paradise," not by
returning to the East, but by advancing to the West.

Columbus understands his dream to be the Lord's reminder
of a secret vow Columbus had made:

> That, if our Princes harkened to my prayer,
> Whatever wealth I brought from that new world
> Should, in this old, be consecrate to lead
> A new crusade against the Saracen,
> And free the Holy Sepulchre from thrall.   (99–103)

The conquest of the East is to be the consequence of wealth
garnered in the movement to the West. Though the Liberal
Anglicans spoke rather of the conversion than the conquest of the
East, they saw that conversion accomplished similarly: because the
earth is a sphere, the spiritual movement of Christianity westward would ultimately produce the conversion of the East. Columbus' search for the East by sailing West becomes for Tennyson an appropriate metaphor to describe the spiritual progress
toward a new paradise, and therefore Columbus can speak of
having "pushed his prows into the setting sun, / And made West
East" (24–25).

It is true, of course, that geographical movement westward is
not in itself a sign of spiritual progress. As Columbus says,

> . . . what a door for scoundrel scum
> I opened to the West, through which the lust,
> Villainy, violence, avarice, of your Spain
> Poured in on all those happy naked isles—   (166–69)

Spiritual progress is dependent upon man's moral choice, but
when a spiritual advance is made by a nation over its predecessors,
that nation is regularly westward. For example, the courts of
Mark and Pellam in *Idylls of the King* are not spiritually advanced over Rome, though they are west of Rome; Arthur's court,
on the other hand, which is spiritually advanced over Rome is
inevitably west. The inevitability of the westward advance of
religion was a lesson which the Liberal Anglicans had learned
from history. Stanley could therefore say, "'Westward the Star
of Empire has held its course,' and westward has the sun of

Christendom moved also." [35] As Forbes points out, "It is significant that Stanley, who travelled in Palestine as a young man, should cross the Atlantic in his old age, full of hope for the future of Christianity," [36] because it was in America, not the Middle East, where he hoped that religion would make its next advance. At any rate, as we have seen, the Liberal Anglicans consistently opposed a flexible and progressive West to a static and degenerate East, and if my reading of Tennyson is correct, he seems to have shared such a view.

Both *Sir John Oldcastle, Lord Cobham* and *Columbus*, then, seem to me to assert the necessity for the westward advance of spiritual progress. The translation of the word and the voyage to the West are used literally and metaphorically to illustrate the necessity for adaptability to change in religion as opposed to reaction. Tennyson had suggested as much in earlier poems—in *Maud* and *Idylls of the King*, for example. Such a belief in both the inevitability and the desirability of change was, as we have seen, at the very core of Liberal Anglican thinking, and it was such a belief which made them oppose most adamantly what they saw as the forces of reaction in the Oxford Movement [37] and in Roman Catholicism. It was also such a belief which made their theology most adaptable to scientific advances, particularly evolutionary theories, which permeated the Victorian world. Though the Oxford Movement was pretty well dead by 1880, the essential controversy between it and Liberal Anglicanism, the controversy between stability, permanence, and ultimately Church authority on the one hand, and evolution, progress, and individual conscience on the other, has been the essential controversy in the Christian Churches from the Reformation to the present time. Far from being historical curiosities, Tennyson's poems seem to me to confront the most relevant contemporary questions.

35. Quoted in Forbes, p. 84.
36. P. 84.
37. Of Thomas Arnold, for example, Charles Sanders says, "In the last analysis, change was a principle of life: 'One would think that people who talk against change were literally as well as metaphorically blind, and really did not see that everything in themselves and around them is changing every hour by the necessary laws of its being.' It is scarcely surprising that Arnold could not come to terms with the reactionary leaders of the Oxford Movement" (*Coleridge and the Broad Church Movement*, p. 109). See also Preyer, "The Oxford Movement and the Germano-Coleridgeans," *Bentham, Coleridge, and the Science of History*, pp. 91–94.

*

Those poems which I have rather loosely grouped as "speculative poems" (for want of a better name) concern themselves either with the reality behind the appearance of things or with the life journey from "out of the deep" to "that last deep where we and thou are still." Both these concerns merge in *The Voyage of Maeldune* (1880), where the life journey takes place on the sea, so often in Tennyson a symbol of the greater reality behind the appearance of things. The allegory of *The Voyage of Maeldune* is clearer and more specific than that of the earlier *The Voyage* (1864) and less personal than that of the later *Merlin and the Gleam* (1889), but all three poems as allegorical treatments of the passage through life are similar. The motivation for the life journey in *The Voyage of Maeldune* is different, however, from the vision or gleam of the other two poems. In *The Voyage of Maeldune,* Maeldune pursues his journey to revenge the murder of his father, but his motivation, taken from Tennyson's source, P. W. Joyce's *Old Celtic Romances,* is less important than the journey itself and the allegorical significance of the isles which he and his men encounter.

There are twelve isles in all, including the one from which Maeldune originally sails, the Isle of Finn. The isles tend to form contrary pairs, e.g., the Silent Isle and the Isle of Shouting, the Isle of Flowers and the Isle of Fruits, the Isle of Fire and the undersea isle, or, in the case of the Isle of the Double Towers, the contrariety is contained in a single isle.[38] The phenomenal world appears again, as it so often does in Tennyson's poetry, as apparently irreconcilable contraries like the light and dark, calm and storm, dawn and sunset, East and West, life and death of other poems.[39] The cycle of life, from the Isle of Finn to the Isle of Finn, confronts these contrarieties in a particular way: all take the form of Isles floating on the Ocean, the Tennysonian symbol of eternal reality. The Ocean here, I think, is the same as "the boundless deep" of the Ancient Sage. The contrary isles are the

38. As Ricks points out in his notes to the *Poems,* "For each pair of islands, Joyce was the source of one; T. elaborated, and provided an antithesis" (p. 1276).

39. This aspect of Tennyson's poetry has received much comment by critics; among the most interesting analyses are Danzig, "The Contraries: A Central Concept in Tennyson's Poetry," and Smith, *The Two Voices.*

appearance, the ocean the eternal reality, and the isles form only a part of the ever changing surface.

The allegorical significance of the various isles is relatively clear. The Silent Isle, marked by the poplar and cypress, traditional symbols of death,[40] where "all of it fair as life" is also "quiet as death" (20), echoes the stasis of living death which Tennyson had dealt with in the same terms in *The Lotos-Eaters*. The Isle of Shouting, its opposite, seems to represent a kind of hysterical, purposeless activity rather than stasis, but the fact that the shouting is done by birds with human voices suggests that the activity is bestial rather than human. Bestial activity, though opposite to the relative inactivity of the Silent Isle, is not therefore preferable to it, and so Maelduae takes his men away. The Isle of Flowers, the next isle, though it is lush and beautiful, is also static. It is free from change but incapable of growth which would produce fruit from flowers.[41] Perhaps Tennyson is again making the point which he had made in the prefatory poem to *The Palace of Art*, that "Beauty, Good, and Knowledge, are three sisters," which "never can be sundered without tears" (10, 13), that, in other words, the beauty of the Isle of Flowers alone is insufficient. The Isle of Fruits is, of course, no better, for if the Isle of Flowers is held always in its spring and middle summer, the Isle of Fruits is apparently always autumn. In both cases the isles are unnatural, as the rhythm of birth, growth, and decay is violated. Tennyson seems to be facing again the problem of change, as he had done in so many early poems and most importantly in *In Memoriam* and concluding again the necessity and essential rightness of it.

The Isle of Fire and the undersea isle are the only isles which seem to appeal to the suicidal in man, for these isles alone cause the mariners to slay themselves rather than attempt to slay each other. And yet the two isles are different: they appeal to radically different kinds of men. The men who throw themselves into the fire do so passionately—"We were giddy besides with the fruits we had gorged, and so crazed that at last / There were some leaped into the fire" (75–76). Those, on the other hand, who

40. Tennyson was apparently familiar with classical and folk traditions which associated the poplar with death, as his use of the poplar to foreshadow death in *Mariana* (1830) would indicate.

41. Cf. *Maud*, Part II, section v, verse viii, where the mad hero dreams of a garden where there are only flowers and no fruits and he associates it with death.

commit suicide at the undersea isle are "three of the gentlest and best of [Maeldune's] people," who seek bliss, Paradise, "quiet fields of eternal sleep" (78–82). Both suicidal tendencies, though oppositely motivated by a crazed activity or a desire for passivity, are equally wrong, and Maeldune sails on. The Bounteous Isle, the next of the islands, pictures a paradisiacal world where there is no necessity to work, that activity which Milton said differentiates men from beasts. As a world without apparent evil, it is a world which necessitates no moral choice and therefore gives no opportunity for moral growth. The isle requires neither action nor endurance through which Julius Hare says one can arrive at the knowledge of spiritual truth.[42] The Isle of Witches seems clearly to suggest the destructive potential of the sexual appetite. The Isle of the Double Towers is perhaps the most ambiguous of the allegorical islands. The two towers, one of "smooth-cut stone" and the other "carved all over with flowers" (106), may refer to any number of contrary factions—religious, aesthetic, even political.[43]

The Isle of a Saint teaches the lesson of reconciliation. It is there that Maeldune is told that vengeance is God's, that he is absolved, and that the ages-long contention between Maeldune's family and the family of the man who killed his father is resolved. The initial contrariety between Maeldune and his enemy ends in reconciliation and Maeldune's return to the Isle of Finn. The theme of the poem seems to be that the choice of either of any two opposites is destructive and that only through spiritual insight, offered here by the saint, can reconciliation be achieved. The circle which Maeldune's journey traces perhaps underscores the cyclical nature of life, but the end of the feud suggests the possibility of a spiritual transcendence.

De Profundis, the second of the speculative poems, written in part at the time of Hallam Tennyson's birth (1852), completed sometime later, and published in 1880, opens with "The Two Greetings," one based on knowledge and the other on wisdom. The first greeting is to the physical human child, the second to

---

42. *The Victory of Faith,* p. 23.

43. Buckley understands the isle to "symbolize religious differences or the clash of science and faith or more generally the inane contentious divisiveness of human society" (*Tennyson,* p. 219).

the divine spiritual child. The first greeting welcomes the child to "this changing world of changeless law" (6) ; he is the perfect child promising the perfect man; he is also the unity formed from the duality of male and female through love. It is hoped that his life will be happy and that it will be a life of service to his fellow man. The first greeting concerns his phenomenal existence and the deep from which he comes seems to be a kind of atomistic reservoir which provides the elements for his material being.

In the second greeting the deep from which the child comes is transformed. It is now the spiritual deep; it is the reality of which our physical world is "but the bounding shore"; it is the reality of which our world is but the "shadow" and the "fleshly sign." Our world of "finite-infinite space / In finite-infinite Time" is but the "mortal veil / And shattered phantom of that infinite One" (45–47). No longer merely an atomistic reservoir from which are drawn the materials of the physical world, the deep becomes the unity of which all in the physical world is the diverse manifestation.

The two worlds thus conceived in the two greetings are not mutually exclusive. The two worlds are conceived of in panentheistic terms. That is, all is God's substance; the child is made by God "Out of His whole World-self and all in all" (49). The spirit is both immanent and transcendent, not merely one or the other. The physical world is a manifestation of God, though in manifesting himself he has at the same time hidden himself, for he is the "light no man can look upon" and is therefore like the child half-lost in his own shadow. Consequently, it is not a matter of which greeting is right or true, for both are right and true. The deep is both physical and spiritual, as the child is both physical and spiritual: the child is the one thing made up of two things— flesh and spirit—as analogically he is the one product of the duality of male and female. The apparent duality of the two worlds from which the two greetings come is only apparent, not real. All is, like the child, one thing. As the concluding section, "The Human Cry," makes clear, God is not the ideal and the phenomenal world the real, for God is both—"for all is Thou and in Thee."

What Tennyson is saying in *De Profundis* is perfectly consistent with what he had said in *In Memoriam*. The phenomenal world is the fleshly sign of the spiritual one. Arthur Hallam is the sign of Christ; the apparent contrarieties of the phenomenal world are the sign for the unity of the spiritual. God is at once the sign and he transcends the sign. The sign is the finite expression of the infinite, but it also partakes of the infinite; it is God but God is not it. The paradox is expressed by the poet in the phrase "this divisible-indivisible world." All is one.

The same panentheistic conception in *De Profundis* is behind *The Higher Pantheism* (1867, 1869), and it is expressed through the same kind of paradox:

> The sun, the moon, the stars, the seas, the hills and
>   the plains—
> Are not these, O Soul, the Vision of Him who reigns?
>
> Is not the Vision He? though He be not that which He
>   seems?
> Dreams are true while they last, and do we not live
>   in dreams?
>
> Earth, these solid stars, this weight of body and limb,
> Are they not sign and symbol of thy division from Him?

Sir Charles Tennyson says that the idea of the poem is "that the material universe, which often seems so menacing and purposeless, may be the vision of God, if not actually a part of God Himself, though man, because of his limited powers, can only get a distorted and partial view of the reality"; [44] and Jerome Buckley says that "the doctrine of appearances he was proposing was not a new pantheism at all but rather a quite consistent theistic idealism." [45] I wish rather to clarify these judgments than to quarrel with them. Panentheism, the doctrine which I think the poem espouses, is a theistic idealism, and not new (though, of course, Tennyson did not call it new, only a higher pantheism). The poem also suggests "that the material universe . . . may be the vision of God, if not actually a part of God himself," though I should delete the qualifications. It seems to me, in other words, that the poem quite clearly states through the form of the rhetorical question that the material universe *is* a vision of God *and* that

44. *Tennyson*, pp. 373–74.
45. *Tennyson*, p. 170.

the vision is a part of God—"Is not the Vision He? though He be not that which He seems?" The vision is God, though God is not limited by the vision. It is precisely this conception which makes the title, *The Higher Pantheism*, relevant. The material universe is God, though God transcends the material universe. The Newtonian image of God's light becoming "broken gleams" in the material world—"Glory about thee, without thee; and thou fulfillest thy doom, / Making Him broken gleams, and a stifled splendour and gloom"—is the same one used in the Prologue to *In Memoriam:*

> Our little systems have their day;
>   They have their day and cease to be:
>   They are but broken lights of thee,
> And thou, O Lord, art more than they.[46]

A similar image is used in the next to the last verse of *The Higher Pantheism:*

> Law is God, say some: no God at all, says the fool;
> For all we have power to see is a straight staff bent
>   in a pool.

The last line of this verse is not, I think, part of what the fool says, but the reason for the fool's error: some say God is law and the fool says there is no God; the fool is led to such a conclusion because our ability to see is limited to God's refracted light. The final lines of the poem reiterate through the rhetorical question the assertion that the Vision is indeed God:

> And the ear of man cannot hear, and the eye of man
>   cannot see;
> But if we could see and hear, this Vision—were it
>   not He?

To deny that the ear can hear or the eye see God is to deny only empirical knowledge of him. God cannot be known, but he can

---

46. Cf. Tennyson's use of the image in *Will Waterproof's Lyrical Monologue* (1842): "Let there be thistles, there are grapes; / If old things, there are new; / Ten thousand broken lights and shapes, / Yet glimpses of the true" (57–60).

be felt; he is perceptible to man's wisdom, but beyond his knowledge. That the material universe, the Vision, is God can be affirmed only "By faith, and faith alone," as Tennyson had said in the Prologue to *In Memoriam,* because wisdom is "Believing where we cannot prove."

Flower in the Crannied Wall, published with *The Higher Pantheism* in *The Holy Grail* volume in 1869, seems also to be a panentheistic speculation, though where *The Higher Pantheism* takes the form of rhetorical questions, *Flower in the Crannied Wall* takes the form of an assertion:

> Flower in the crannied wall,
> I pluck you out of the crannies,
> I hold you here, root and all, in my hand,
> Little flower—but *if* I could understand
> What you are, root and all, and all in all,
> I should know what God and man is.

To suggest that if one could understand a flower he would then know both God and man is at once to assert the existence of God and to deny the possibility of knowledge of him.[47] One cannot, of course, understand the flower, but if he could, he would know not only what God is, but what man is, because man and the flower presumably are one and both are one with God. All appearances are reconciled in the spirit though knowledge of such reconciliation is unavailable to us; we cannot *know* it but we can believe it.

By 1869 Tennyson had apparently speculated in a more systematic way upon metaphysics than he had by 1850. He may have been encouraged to this by his association with the "Metaphysical Society," founded in part by him in 1869.[48] The more systematic

47. Tennyson is probably careful to use the verb *understand* here, as I think that he would make the same distinction between reason and understanding that Coleridge makes. (See Sanders' discussion of reason and understanding and their relation to the Broad Church in *Coleridge and the Broad Church Movement,* pp. 35–48.) Tennyson does not, however, usually refer to these two powers as reason and understanding, but rather refers to their matter as knowledge and wisdom and often describes the approach to them as knowing and feeling.

48. See *Memoir,* pp. 556–61. At the first regular meeting of the society James Knowles read *The Higher Pantheism.* Tennyson did not attend. See Sir Charles Tennyson, *Tennyson,* p. 381.

panentheism of *The Higher Pantheism* and *De Profundis,* however, is in no way inconsistent with the "metaphysics" of *In
Memoriam.*[49] Tennyson had all along felt, perhaps rather vaguely,
that the divine was housed somehow in the person of Arthur Hallam and that the apparent contrarieties of nature could somehow
be reconciled through faith in the spirit which lay behind them.
It was not until the writing of *De Profundis,* however, that the
divisibility–indivisibility of God from nature apparently suggested itself to him in panentheistic terms. The difference between
Arthur Hallam as the personal form through which the persona
of *In Memoriam* could contemplate celestial truths, as a being
who in death fused with Christ, and an Arthur Hallam as both
God and not God, is perhaps small. Tennyson's panentheism of
the later poems, in other words, is rather an extension of his
speculations on the material universe and the spirit behind it than
a divergence from them. It is perhaps fortunate that Tennyson's
theistic idealism had not become more systematic, however hypothetical, by 1850, or the lyricism of a long poem such as *In
Memoriam* might have given way to exposition.

*

We have long regarded Tennyson as "Schoolmiss Alfred" or
"Alfred Lawn Tennyson"; we have looked upon him as a mind-
less emotional poet, a diarist, at his best a lyrical poet of some
genius but little intellect. We have accused him of shallow
chauvinism or of playing the role of *sacer vates* for money or for
vanity. And yet all of these responses to Tennyson seem to me to
be in error, occasioned perhaps by the difficulty of looking upon
the Victorian period with an unprejudiced eye. The Victorian
world is now opening to us, however, and at a sufficient distance

---

49. Tennyson seems to have been generally consistent in this regard: Cf. the
following lines from *Locksley Hall Sixty Years After,* published in 1886:

> Only That which made us, meant us to be mightier by and by,
> Set the sphere of all the boundless Heavens within the human eye,

> Sent the shadow of Himself, the boundless, through the human soul;
> Boundless inward, in the atom, boundless outward, in the Whole.

(209–12)

so that a more positive and more accurate judgment can be made. We can now see that Tennyson is one of many spokesmen for the age, but not in the narrow, complacent, or superficial way that we thought he was. He addresses the problems that were real for the Victorians and are real for us, and he addresses them in a thoughtful and often profound way, whether we agree with his responses or not. They are, of course, the responses of the artist, for like Hardy, who described his own art as "an endeavour to give shape and coherence to a series of seemings, or personal impressions," Tennyson is an artist, not a philosopher. But he is no less thoughtful and thought-provoking because his work is not philosophy, but art. If it is true that we cannot understand the present unless we understand the past, it is to our interest to seek to understand Tennyson. And for that, we need only listen to what he says.

Index